LOST
AT SEA

LOST
AT SEA

POVERTY AND PARADISE COLLIDE
AT THE EDGE OF AMERICA

JOE KLOC

DEYST.
An Imprint of William Morrow

HarperCollins books may be purchased for educational, business, or sales promotional use. For information, please email the Special Markets Department at SPsales@harpercollins.com.

FIRST EDITION

Designed by Alison Bloomer

Library of Congress Cataloging-in-Publication Data has been applied for.

ISBN 978-0-06-306169-9

25 26 27 28 29 LBC 5 4 3 2 1

FOR MOM

I am a true adorer of life, and if I can't reach as high as the face of it, I plant my kiss somewhere lower down.

—SAUL BELLOW, *Henderson the Rain King*

CONTENTS

AUTHOR'S NOTE

THE ANCHOR-OUTS ARE CLASSIFIED AS "HOMELESS" BY THE MARIN County Department of Health and Human Services. The diversity of the community challenges that definition: while some live in dire poverty, suffer many of the same ailments common among the chronically unhoused, and live on unseaworthy vessels simply to have a roof over their heads, others hold down jobs, have retirement pensions, and could secure housing but have no desire to do so. With regards to the anchor-outs, this book uses the terms "homeless" and, when referring to specific people, "unhoused" for two reasons: first, because many of the policies directed at the community conceive of it that way; and second, because as the book progresses through the years, the description unfortunately becomes more proximal to the truth. But ultimately it is flawed.

Likewise, the national unhoused population is not in all ways represented by the anchor-outs. Only about half of the US unhoused population is white, whereas the vast majority of the anchor-outs are. This difference may in part be due to the demographics of Sausalito itself, where over 90 percent of the residents are white. This demographic is in part a function of the fact that during World War II, when thousands of southern Black laborers arrived for work at the shipyards, they were unable to join unions, given lower-paying jobs, and denied access to both loans and home-buying opportunities in the city. Many went instead to neighboring Marin City, which today is 26 percent Black. It shares a zip code with Sausalito, but not a budget.

Lastly, in Sausalito, the residents serving on the city council, including in the role of mayor, change to some extent on a yearly basis, subject to elections. For this reason, when referring to their words and actions, this book does not attempt to identify and introduce each member by name but only by his or her position. As the reader will see, the political will of the council has remained consistent, regardless of the individual officeholders at any given moment. In places, transcripts of their meetings are edited for clarity and length.

LOST
AT SEA

INTRODUCTION

THIS IS A STORY ABOUT PEOPLE WHO, FOR ONE REASON OR ANOTHER, HAVE come to live on abandoned vessels anchored in the waters of Richardson Bay, a two-square-mile saltwater estuary just north of San Francisco. Among them are retired mariners, single mothers, runaways, artists, addicts, and many others who caught a bad break from which they haven't yet recovered: a divorce, a lost job, a jail sentence. There are those who hope their pasts won't find them, and those who wish they would. With little or no money in their pockets, they make their way together on the water. Some grow vegetables in ten-gallon buckets and trade them for a helping hand from seasoned live-aboards who know how to patch a hull after a winter storm. Others look after the children whose parents must take the bus down to San Francisco or up to San Rafael to work an odd job or receive treatment for a stubborn ache or cough. The elders, some of whom are in their nineties, use their Social Security checks and military pensions to buy hot dogs and whiskey to feed the congregation of the Pirate Church, a gathering of worshipers who meet each week on the patio outside the public library to stand atop picnic tables and read from the Torah and the New Testament about the promise of days to come.

This community, known as the anchor-outs, dates back at least to the Earthquake and Fire of 1906, but many consider themselves heirs to much older histories: to the early days of the Gold Rush, when prospectors came in search of luck and found none; or to the days when Alta California was Mexican, and Spanish before that, when the sea captain from whom the bay takes its name first sold fresh water to sailors seeking refuge on their way up the then-uncharted Pacific Coast; or to the Coast Miwok, the original inhabitants of the Marin Hills who sailed and traded along those waters, whose way of life was ruined in different ways by each successive group's arrival, and about whom no record has been found to indicate that, in their three-thousand-year history, they ever sought war.

In 1969, the US Congress declared the estuary to be a federal special anchorage, formally establishing it as a protected refuge for sailors in the choppy North Pacific where they could drop anchor, wait out a storm, make repairs, and resupply for their journey ahead. The anchor-outs see themselves as no different from any other seafarers in need of safe harbor. But this is not the view on land. Many who live in the surrounding communities, particularly those in the wealthy shoreside city of Sausalito, consider the anchor-outs freeloaders who avoid taxes, clog up the channel, and pollute the waters of the estuary.

Sausalito's animosity toward the anchor-outs has ebbed and flowed with the makeup of its city council, whose five members are elected to staggered four-year terms. When, in the 1980s, the political winds shifted, a plan was put in place to clear the anchorage. Sausalito and the other municipalities of the bay consolidated their jurisdictions into what became known as the Richardson Bay Regional Agency (RBRA). They passed ordinances limiting the time a vessel could anchor in the water to seventy-two hours and hired a harbormaster to enforce them. Some anchor-outs complied and vanished from the anchorage, but many others ignored the new rules, in certain cases for more than a quarter of a century. The RBRA, underfunded and uncertain of its own legal footing, had little ability to press the issue, beyond the issuance of the occasional ticket here or there. In this way, the anchor-outs and the Sausalitans coexisted for many years in a quiet stalemate, at times forgetting they were even at odds at all.

WHEN I FIRST HEARD OF THE anchor-outs, in the summer of 2010, I had just moved to San Francisco from New York. The community was mentioned in passing by a friend who thought the anchorage would make a good story for me to report: a tale of eccentrics living peacefully off the grid in one of the richest counties in America. The local press agreed, referring to the community as a tradition to be tolerated, if not always embraced. The city's biggest complaint back then was that the anchor-outs' anchors dragged on the bay floor, killing off patches of the protected eelgrass that provided shelter for young fish and oxygenated the bay. I didn't pursue the story, but over the next few years several events would draw my attention back to Richardson Bay. The first was the emergence of the Occupy movement in the fall of 2011, when hundreds of thousands of people in more than six hundred US cities protested the country's growing income inequality. On nights when I camped in Oscar Grant Plaza in Oakland, watching volunteers struggle to feed hundreds of people sleeping in tents as police surrounded the park and readied their tear gas, my mind drifted to the anchor-outs. I wondered if their community was really the floating paradise I'd believed it to be.

My image of the anchorage was further complicated a year later, in 2012, after I had returned to New York. I'd gotten to know an unhoused man in his sixties who passed his evenings on a bench in Greenwich Village's Christopher Park. He told me that he'd spent his life wandering the world, moving from one city to the next in Europe and Asia, earning pocket money by offering unsuspecting visitors English-language tours of whatever place he happened to find himself in. But he was old now, and he felt it was time to return home. "I never made new roots," he said. "So I had to come back." When I asked him why he thought that he hadn't settled down, he just shrugged and directed me to the introduction to one of his favorite books, Edmund Love's *Subways Are for Sleeping*. Published in 1957, Love's book profiled a handful of unhoused New Yorkers in the 1950s who had survived on the streets for many years. "Most of them are in a state of reassessment," Love wrote.

They have come up against something which they cannot understand, and which they want to think about. The thinking is important to them. [They] are living stop gap lives. They are waiting for the big break. That break may be a call from the producer of a Broadway show. It may be a horse that gallops home at 40–1. It may be just a bright and shining light that suddenly comes to show them the way out of the jungle. Some aren't sure what kind of a break they are waiting for, but they have assured me that they will recognize it when it comes.

Reading Love's book, I began to consider that poverty alone might not fully explain the circumstances of longtime anchor-outs. The majority of the more than 600,000 people in the United States living without shelter at any given moment will regain their footing within the year and recover from their financial calamity. But the troubles of the almost 150,000 who are chronically homeless, as is the case with many in Richardson Bay, can be harder to pin down. Some are burdened with mental illness and addiction, but for others, like the man I got to know in Christopher Park, the causes are less straightforward. As Love wrote, "They wait and try to keep going through today, for tomorrow may bring the miracle." One night sitting on that park bench in the Village, I asked my unhoused friend what he thought about being stuck always in a state of waiting. "Music is notes and blanks," he told me. "My life has a lot of blanks."

We all have blanks. But to inhabit them so completely—as the anchor-outs do, floating for years in derelict boats at the edge of the continent—was another matter entirely. I wanted to understand. And so, in the spring of 2015, I took the first of what would turn out to be many trips to Richardson Bay over the next eight years, the accounts of which make up this story. Over the time in which the book unfolds, the lives and views of the anchor-outs would come to be transformed not only by Sausalito and the RBRA but by the elections of Donald Trump and Joe Biden, by the coronavirus pandemic, and by the epidemic of homelessness in California, which grew by 57 percent between 2015 and the start of 2024.

AT THE BOOK'S OUTSET, WHEN I arrived in Sausalito in 2015, the city's fragile truce with the anchor-outs was beginning to crumble. The same forces that had grown the bank accounts of its most affluent residents were now pushing more and more Americans into poverty: while the S&P 500 was up more than 60 percent from the months before the Great Recession, the number of unhoused people in San Francisco had increased by 16 percent, to over 7,500. Like many wealthy municipalities in California, Sausalito had long refused to build shelters and soup kitchens, incentivizing those living on the streets to concentrate elsewhere in impoverished urban enclaves like Skid Row in Los Angeles and the Tenderloin in San Francisco. For decades, the approach worked, and the city's homeless population was contained, bobbing at a distance. But by 2015, the strategy was failing. Years of stagnant wages, home foreclosures, and lost jobs had grown the anchorage population to well over two hundred people. Homelessness was transforming Sausalito, and a new, more aggressive stance toward the people of Richardson Bay was starting to take shape.

For much of its history, Sausalito has been a place of considerable wealth. Many of its residents live in leafy Victorian mansions built a century ago by San Francisco's monied class, whose families inherited their fortunes directly or indirectly from mining and water barons. Others occupy more modern homes, built with the gains from the many real estate, agriculture, and technology booms that have occurred so frequently around their inlet of the Pacific Ocean. There are also residents, of more modest means, whose neighborhoods were built in the late nineteenth century by Portuguese immigrants from the Azores; these neighborhoods were also inhabited by the shipbuilders of World War II who worked in the city's Marinship Yard, the most productive shipyard of the war effort. But in the past few decades their ranks have been shrinking. One recent study of Marin County—where the median home value was about $1.1 million—found that, while 45 percent of longtime employees of the county can afford to have homes in the city where they work, only 25 percent of new hires can. After the Great Recession, the number of residents living in RVs or on the streets began to grow. Over a three-year period, chronic homelessness increased 36 percent. In turn, the size of the anchorage, which had remained stable at around one hundred vessels for decades, had doubled by the mid-2010s.

By then, more and more anchor-outs had begun to gather at the local park and outside the 7-Eleven, filling the sidewalks and outdoor cafés with their hiking backpacks and flip-phone chargers and crowding the docks with dinghies and kayaks. Their visibility only hardened Sausalito's resolve to evict them: anchor-outs were ticketed and jailed for minor infractions, and their floating homes were declared to be marine debris, towed to the Army Corps of Engineers yard, and crushed, often with decades of personal belongings and family heirlooms inside. In the time over which this book unfolds, anchor-outs who once described their world to me as "an ever-living society gumbo" grew paranoid toward one another. Violence among them became more commonplace. No one any longer spoke of plans to fix up their boat, of the big break just around the corner. And the holy men who once preached salvation and glory for those who lived outside of money now preached only of the coming apocalypse for the unhoused people of Richardson Bay. They saw it long before I did.

THE EPIDEMIC OF HOMELESSNESS IS NOT unique to Sausalito and is spreading both across the nation and in the state of California: as of 2024, the number of unhoused people in the United States was estimated to be about 650,000, and 28 percent of them resided in California. About three-quarters of unhoused people in the United States did not become unhoused as the result of a serious illness, like schizophrenia, but rather, in most cases, as a result of their area's chronic shortage of affordable housing. The consequences of homelessness, however, are substance misuse, depression, suicidal thoughts, and symptoms of trauma, brought on in part by, as one 2020 study put it, "the daily struggles and emotional toll of exposure not only to the elements but to scorn and harassment from passers-by and the police." More than half of the unhoused population of the United States has suffered a traumatic brain injury while living on the street.

This story of the anchor-outs is uniquely suited to revealing certain of the mechanics of homelessness. Both the anchorage and Sausalito can trace their origins to the development, almost entirely within the past 170 years, of San Francisco, a relatively small major city. The same fortunes, powers, and policies drove the growth of each population, side by side, toward opposite fates. For example, the profits that historically built Sausalito were primarily generated by the mining and real estate industries. The environmental negligence of these industries was so great, and had endangered the San Francisco Bay waterway so severely, that the state of California was forced to pass legislation to thwart them. Only a decade later, local and regional authorities began using that very same law to clear the waterfront of unhoused people, to make way for new real estate developments.

It is a long story, and a central one of this book. But it is neither the only story nor the most important: first and foremost, this is an account of the lives of people living on the anchorage. It documents their traditions, their churches, their celebrations, their feuds, their relationships, and their jokes at a time when they were under the greatest threat of their one-hundred-year existence. It is the story of what we all stand to destroy when unhoused and low-income communities are allowed to be flattened out of their humanity and peculiarity, to be torn apart by ill-considered, profit-driven policies that ask them to pick up and move along, as if, in tearing down camp and scattering in all directions, they have nothing left to lose.

PART 1

THE CALM
2015–2016

1

WHEN THE WATER WAS CALM AND THE HARBORMASTER WAS AWAY, THE anchor-outs filled their backpacks with tobacco and sandwiches and rowed their boats to shore. They tied up in the shade of a box elder and went about their day in Dunphy Park, a three-and-a-half-acre patch of grass a mile up the Sausalito coastline. It was a peaceful place. On the north end, there was an old decaying ship, known as the *Galilee*, where egrets hunted herring in the eelgrass. Near the water's edge was a small white gazebo with a gently sloping roof under which anchor-outs married and mourned the loss of loved ones at long last carried out by the tide. If the sun was shining, the anchor-outs stretched out with their dogs beneath the willows to trade leftovers and gossip: about a vanished neighbor, an ill-tempered new arrival, an attack on them in the local paper. In this way they took in these quiet moments and readied themselves as best they could for whatever storm blew through next. They were easy to spot among the residents of Sausalito. They were often rolling cigarettes and bickering like old friends. And they looked tired, maybe from a night in jail or a fight with the police that had left them battered and hunched over, disabused of the value of posturing.

One afternoon, in the spring of 2015, I went down the shoreline of Dunphy Park in search of an anchor-out I knew named Innate Thought. Rumor was that the Coast Guard had raided his boat and now he was demanding redress from the Supreme Court. This otherwise fantastical claim was, in Innate's case, at least conceivable: he was a self-taught anchorage lawyer with an encyclopedic knowledge of American maritime jurisprudence that he dispensed freely and often to his neighbors, without regard to solicitation. But no one had yet seen him that day; of late, I was told in the park, he'd been holed up on his boat, editing a documentary about Richardson Bay on a laptop he'd wired to a car battery.

Having no luck finding him, I stood along the water. The air was quiet but for the honking of gulls and the clamoring of jib hanks when the breeze blew across the bay.

An anchor-out in a white linen robe with curly black locks approached me. He introduced himself as Jeff Jacob. He was a Jubilee Messenger, he said.

Jubilee? I asked.

Every fiftieth year, according to the Book of Leviticus, the debts of the poor vanish as the lonely are reunited with their families and all property is restored to its rightful owners. And during that year the people finally rest, needing neither to reap nor to sow, for God in the twelve months prior will have made their crops bountiful. Scripture says that the Jubilee was observed at least as far back as the time of Jacob and was handed down centuries later from Noah to Moses. On the seventh month of the fiftieth year, said God to Moses atop Mount Sinai, he must blow the trumpet on the Day of Atonement and proclaim liberty throughout the land to all its inhabitants.

I looked west, to the Sausalito hillside dotted with three-story mansions painted in soft pinks and blues. Then, over by the gazebo, I spotted Innate's older brother, Dream Weaver, and watched as he tossed a ball for his pit bull, Bleau Bell, and coughed into his sleeve. When I turned back to Jeff, he'd already wandered off down the beach.

"HEY, BROTHER!" I HEARD SOMEONE CALL in my direction. It was Innate, at last, waving to me to join him on a nearby park bench.

He introduced me to his partner, Melissa, who'd moved to the anchorage from Hawaii only a year before. He packed a glass bowl with weed and hit it with a lighter he kept tied around his neck. Smoke billowed from his mouth as he passed it to a large older man covered in paint.

"This is Bo," Innate said.

I recognized the name. Off and on, Bo had been around Richardson Bay for half a century. He collected driftwood on which he painted seascapes with dried-out brushes and straws. He left them scattered about town, in front of the public library, in the 7-Eleven parking lot, and outside the gas station. The works were free for the taking, but for ten dollars he would add his signature: *VanBo.*

Bo fished a can of Steel Reserve from the plastic bucket tied to the handlebars of his bicycle. He took a sip and switched on a portable radio. Something's off, he told us, looking out across the park. Not long ago he'd had a confrontation with the Sausalito police that he couldn't figure out. "I was out there fucking with the boat," he said, when officers, who have jurisdiction over the westernmost portion of the anchorage, boarded his vessel and handcuffed him.

Dream, who'd been listening at a distance, walked over and asked Bo what cause the police provided for the arrest.

Bo sighed. "For resisting arrest."

Innate shook his head and passed the bowl back to Bo.

Sam Smith's "Stay with Me" came on the radio.

"They can't eradicate us!" Innate shouted.

Everyone grumbled.

Innate exhaled. "They have to take us one by one," he whispered to himself. He turned to me: "There are hardships out there right now. I got a ticket for being in a rowboat while not having a life preserver."

As I learned, the problem wasn't so much the tickets or the nights in jail; it was what might happen to their boats when they were in court or incarcerated. If a harbormaster finds an empty boat,

Innate said, "he might say it's adrift, crush it. Or if it's still a good boat, he might take it up to Petaluma and sell it on Craigslist."

Dream laughed. "Well, that's a good lesson. You need to learn that! Be prepared for the assholes."

Life on the water hadn't always been this rough. In the 1980s, even after Sausalito and the other municipalities of the bay formed the Richardson Bay Regional Agency (RBRA) and published their seventy-two-hour ordinance, they enforced it sparingly. The anchorage was a jurisdictional mess: it was created by the US Congress and placed in the care of the Coast Guard with no constraints on the duration of time a vessel could stay. At the state level, it was governed by the Bay Conservation and Development Commission (BCDC). Established to preserve the habitat of the San Francisco Bay waterway, the commission derived its authority from an environmental protection act passed in 1965 by the California State Legislature. In turn, the BCDC had vested the RBRA with its enforcement powers. Whether this patched-together framework allowed the RBRA or the Sausalito police to evict an unhoused person had never been tested in court. And for decades, with the size of the anchorage holding steady at about one hundred people, the RBRA didn't appear eager to find out. But following the Great Recession, as the number of people in the estuary more than doubled, the harbormaster had grown increasingly aggressive. His concerns took on an environmental flavor: anchor-outs were killing eelgrass with their lines, he argued, and polluting the water with feces and trash. To Innate, the latter charge was the most egregious: the city of Sausalito had ended the practice of sending around a boat to collect their trash and pump out their storage tanks, and now the city was penalizing them for what happened as a result.

Bo stood up and pointed southward, toward a patch of tall grass jutting out into the water. Behind it was a yacht club, where members strolled along the docks, past the ninety-foot berths and pump-out stations, the laundry machines and warm showers.

"This used to be an Indian graveyard," he said. "Now people build buildings where they stole the land. Burned it. And now they're walking on it. Then it used to be a shipyard where they built ships for the Army. It happened again. They gave the Indians beads for land, then they gave the Black guys crack. Then they sold out to guys with pointed shoes and tight jackets. Just go downtown."

I looked over to Innate, whose chin was on his chest, swallowed by the stretched-out neck of his crackled old graphic T-shirt.

Did he ever dream of moving back onto land? Of getting free of the harbormaster?

No, he said. He'd learned to love himself on the water. And anyway, rich people all go to hell.

But didn't he miss his life as an IT worker in San Diego, with his warm bed and steady income?

"That's not what makes me smile," he said. "The happiness I get comes from the toil."

LATER, AS THE SKY TURNED TO orange, Bo noticed a young girl, maybe five years old, running across the grass, looking for someone to play with before the sun dropped behind the hill. He grabbed a Frisbee from the ground and tossed it her way.

After a couple of throws, the Frisbee landed on the roof of the gazebo. Bo, now a few Steel Reserves in, stumbled over to the nearby gravel lot and picked up a harpoon. It was maybe six feet long, with a rusted hook on the end. He swung it wildly at the gazebo's roof, attempting to snag the errant disc.

A man in khaki shorts and a polo shirt asked him to stop. He sounded exhausted, like he'd had the conversation many times before.

Bo ignored him. Eventually, though, he abandoned his efforts anyway, dropping the harpoon in the grass. After he stumbled away, the girl resolved to continue the recovery operation and attempted to lift the spear herself.

The man in khaki shorts told her to leave the spear alone.

She giggled and pulled at the handle.

To no one in particular the man demanded to know who the child's parents were.

On a bench by the shore, a group of anchor-outs watched the five-year-old's obviously futile attempts to lift the heavy harpoon, confused by the urgency of the man's concern. But after other Sausalitans took notice and began to crowd around the gazebo, an old woman on the bench shouted: "Put it down!"

The child jumped to attention, dropped the handle, and ran off toward the beach.

Satisfied, the Sausalitans disbanded. Some returned to their games of bocce ball, while others headed out for dinner at one or another of the restaurants along the shore.

The anchor-outs on the bench resumed their evening, peeling clementines for one another, exchanging copies of the paper, complaining of all the ways in which local columnists failed to get their story right.

The old woman exhaled. The day's trouble had passed. She took another hit off her joint.

Beside me, Innate began to laugh.

I recalled to him something that Bo had said: "Everyone can't live in the same place."

He nodded.

Did the Coast Guard really raid your boat? I asked.

They had, he told me. But they'd made a mistake in allowing Sausalito police officers to join them. According to his interpretation of a recent Supreme Court ruling about a houseboat in Florida, no city official had a right to board his barge.

So he was suing for damages?

Innate sighed. This wasn't about money or his boat. This was his chance to stop the anchorage from being destroyed.

I looked out at the hundreds of boats bobbing in the bay, just as they had done for almost a century. This was what being on the verge of destruction looked like?

He shook his head. I wasn't seeing it. Something big was happening. But he didn't have time to explain. He needed to get back to his boat before the tide went out and a sandbar blocked his passage. Next time I was around, he said, I should drop by and he'd explain everything.

By now it was almost dark.

As he made for his dinghy he flashed his hard-earned yellow smile: "When you pick away the crust," he said, "the pudding comes out."

2

THAT NIGHT, BACK IN MY HOTEL ROOM IN SAN FRANCISCO, I THOUGHT OF what Jeff had said about the Jubilee.

Many biblical scholars, including Jeff, believe that the Jubilee is the key to understanding a mysterious line from Moses in the Book of Genesis: "And the Lord said, 'My spirit shall not strive with man forever, for he is indeed flesh; yet his days shall be *one hundred and twenty years.*'"

If Adam lived to 930 years of age, Noah to 950, and his son Shem to 600, then what did God mean when he limited man's days to 120 years? After all, it was only a few decades ago, in 1997, that Jeanne Calment, a French woman who prayed each morning and smoked for a century, died at the age of 122.

It's been theorized instead that God was speaking in Jubilee years and referring not to the life span of individuals but to that of all humankind; he was declaring that people will inhabit the earth for 120 Jubilees, or 6,000 years from the time of creation, when Adam and Eve were expelled from Eden. To know when the world ends, then, one only needs to know of its beginning.

The Coast Miwok were the first inhabitants of the land now called Sausalito. They tell us that before the earth there was only water and a silver fox who was walking aimlessly in the fog, singing her prayer to a now-lost melody: "I want to meet someone." When a coyote appeared, she told him she was lonely, and so they decided to walk together, though they had no place to go. "Let's make the world," Silver Fox said at an unknown date. But Coyote didn't know how to make a world. "We will sing," she told him, and her lonely prayer at once became the song of sod and mud as she and Coyote danced and the earth formed beneath their feet. Up first from the vast waters rose the peak of Won-nah-pi's, which, on a distant day, certain of the ancestors of those soon to be made by Coyote and Silver Fox would call Sonoma Mountain. Coyote unfurled across the water great mats of sewn-together sticks and leaves, upon which he planted trees and built up mountains. He made different types of creatures from different types of feathers and different types of sticks. Some would be drawn to the water's edge of their new earth, to collect shells and fish and paddle the oceans. Others journeyed inland, to hunt in the forests and climb the mountainsides. In these ways all people were made. They scattered across the earth, each in search of home, and soon forgot where they had begun. Those who stayed put, in what is now called Marin County, became the Coast Miwok. They taught themselves to fish steelhead and salmon from the rivers and creeks that snaked down the hillsides into San Francisco Bay; to trap rabbits and hunt antelope and deer; and to gather acorns and store them in granaries they built from bark found in the redwood forests, which must have seemed old even then. When the tides of the Pacific beached a whale, they cut out its blubber. They also dug mollusks from the sand along the water. After the meat was licked clean, they tossed the shells in great mounds, which sometimes grew to hundreds of feet in diameter. They made beads from the clam shells, to use as money with neighboring villages and tribes of California. In our time, no tool or weapon has been unearthed to indicate that they ever went to war, or even considered it. No songs of battle have been passed down. For thousands of years, everyone slept easy and cherished feathers, for feathers were what Coyote used to make people.

As Bo had explained to me in the park, many anchor-outs traced their way of life back to the Coast Miwok. Anchor-outs were peaceful and lived among the estuary's terns and rays and herring, trading their vegetables and hard work freely, without interest in owning anything. When an unhoused person showed up on their shores in search of shelter, they helped them salvage an abandoned vessel in their charge. It was not that every anchor-out had wanted to spend their nights in the chilly hull of a leaky boat, but Sausalito gave them no other choice: each year since 2007, when the state of California had mandated that the Sausalito City Council take up the issue of rezoning for the construction of a homeless shelter, the city had demurred. For those with nowhere to sleep, the anchorage was their only hope.

THAT FEBRUARY THE COUNCIL ONCE AGAIN gathered to address the state's shelter mandate.

The five members, including the mayor, met as they always did in a small room inside the Sausalito Civic Center, a converted century-old schoolhouse that was built at the end of the nineteenth century halfway up the city's coastline, in the neighborhood known as New Town. The building also houses the library and the historical society's archives, and it was not uncommon to see anchor-outs walking the halls, on their way to tracking down an ordinance, visiting a computer to check for messages from lawyers and loved ones, or attending a council meeting and availing themselves of the opportunity to issue a public comment, as they often did when the issue of the shelters was again raised.

The mayor called the meeting to order, and the city clerk took the podium.

Eight years earlier, the clerk explained, California's legislature had passed a law aimed at increasing the number of available shelter beds. At the time the bill was drawn up, the number of unhoused Californians was about 360,000, or almost two-thirds of the population of Wyoming. Its drafters argued that, because smaller, wealthier communities like Sausalito zoned themselves in such a way as to prohibit the construction of shelters, their unhoused residents were forced to migrate to large and overcrowded urban encampments, like Skid Row in Los Angeles and the Tenderloin in San Francisco. This depleted the resources for unhoused people in these urban enclaves, causing their living conditions to deteriorate even further. The law ordered Sausalito to zone a parcel of land to accommodate the construction of a shelter, should one be deemed necessary.

"This is not something we just decided," the mayor explained from the dais, which stood in front of a painting of the Golden Gate Bridge connecting Marin County to San Francisco. "This is required by law. We have to do it."

Attendance was high, with many Sausalitans eager to voice their opposition to the proposed shelter sites.

"I know some people are concerned," the mayor added. "We are a long way away from having any shelters on city property."

"Mr. Mayor," said another council member, "could we perhaps get public comment?"

A woman in a sweater approached the podium.

"Are you ready for me?" she asked. "I live in the north end of town next to the schools. I've spent the last few days talking to everyone in my neighborhood. We're very unclear about this. What is an emergency shelter? Most of us were under the impression that it was emergency housing. Which is great. Great. We need emergency housing for floods or earthquakes. But what concerns us is the treatment center aspect of it. I'll be really succinct about that. We are concerned about this being in our neighborhood, in our schools, next to our kids. Fifty-nine people in a treatment center for nine months? Who is going to be in these treatment centers? I'm a member of Alcoholics Anonymous, and I have been for twenty years. I've spent a lot of time on the street level in this town, helping people. When your sisters and your brothers and your family need someone to come, I go. I do that in Sausalito. So I'm very keen on homeless shelters. I don't have anything against homeless centers. I don't have anything against people trying to get their lives together. I help people all the time trying to get their lives together. I have an issue with it at the schools and on *my* street—because I'm selfish."

Several more speakers echoed her concerns.

One called the state's mandate "an overreach" of state government.

Another opposed a proposed zoning site's proximity to a school: "I don't think anyone is trying to discard these people's lives and needs, but the fundamental issue is taking it to the kids." The man was apparently unaware that about one in thirty children in America face homelessness each year. He was hardly alone in his misconceptions. For instance, though it is often believed that the unhoused don't want to work, around 40 percent of people living without shelter are employed, either full- or part-time. Many live on the streets because they can't afford housing in the communities where they have jobs and familial ties. Their options are limited: the United States has shelter beds for only about one in twenty unhoused people. The California legislature's bill to which the man was opposed was an effort to close this very gap.

A man in a suit and tie explained that his problem with the city building a shelter was that "it's only for the homeless, the chronically ill, abusers, and things like that. So it's not for the residents."

The room clapped, as it had after each speaker.

A mild-mannered man approached the microphone.

"Hello," he said, removing his glasses. "I want to make a broader observation. Whenever these state mandates come along, typically there are a lot of complaints. And whether we are talking about providing zoning for a homeless shelter or a mandate to provide zoning for affordable housing, oftentimes there are complaints that this heavy-handed one-size-fits-all approach doesn't take into account our unique community attributes. And fair enough. But Sausalito historically has had a lot of affordable housing. And that's greatly diminished today. And it's declining steadily. And for as long as I have been here, twenty-six years, we've had a homeless population, as well as a significant near-homeless population—I'm referring to some of the anchor-outs who are on boats that barely float. So what I'd like to see us as a community do—however you resolve this—is that once we resolve this state mandate, wouldn't it be great if we actually had a conversation as a community: What kind of community do we want to be in twenty-five, fifty years? Do we want to still be an economically diverse community, or do we want to slowly evolve into a community that is only for the wealthy?"

This evolution, however, was arguably all but complete already. With the average home price in Sausalito above $1 million, many working-class people were excluded from obtaining not only a place to live inside the city but also the address they needed to have a vote in who sat on the city council. That's not to say that working-class people weren't around, waiting tables, washing dishes. But each night, when the shops turned out their lights, they gathered downtown and waited for the bus to take them back across the Golden Gate Bridge. Sometimes I rode the buses with them, on my way back to one or another friend's apartment. By the time we reached the bridge it would always be quiet. Where they went from our stop in San Francisco I couldn't say. But some, no doubt, still had at least another hour on their journey, a train ride over to the East Bay, to more affordable housing where, with any luck, they could spend a bit of time with their families and rest, before waking up the next day to do it all over again.

Life along the western shore of Richardson Bay had not always been this way. Seventy years earlier, World War II had brought thousands of workers to the Marinship Yard to weld and rivet together Liberty ships and balloon barges. Before that, Portuguese shipbuilders lived and toiled on the muddy waterfront. But the march of wealth had always moved in one direction: for hundreds of years, the haves imposed their will on the have-nots, not only shaping and reshaping Sausalito but creating the city itself.

The transformation of the area began around the turn of the eighteenth century, when the Spanish Crown ordered the viceroy of New Spain to sail to California in search of more treasure. A Jesuit expedition did just that and returned to announce, to the viceroy's astonishment, that California was not an island at all but connected by land to their new empire. The Spaniards had known this once, a hundred years before, but forgotten it in the commotion of conquest. They built grand adobe missions and presidios in Baja California, in San Diego, and by 1770 as far north as Monterey. Six years later, a ship of monks on a voyage to Monterey overshot the settlement and wound up among the Coast Miwok of San Francisco Bay. They brought back tales of the foggy safe harbor, of the redwood forests, the fields of mint, the freshwater springs, and the great shell mounds they had happened upon. In June 1776, a Spanish expedition returned to the bay and built a mission not far from a small freshwater lagoon. Soldiers arrived in August with cattle, horses, mules, and sheep. Only four months passed before the first of the Coast Miwok people were baptized at the mission by the lagoon, which the Spanish had named Dolores, after Mater Dolorosa, to honor the sorrows of life. Spain named the settlement Yerba Buena and granted the monks complete authority over all the inhabitants.

The monks built their missions on tracts of fertile land where they raised thousands of heads of cattle. For worship they built churches with marble altars finished with gold and silver. They surrounded those churches with homes for themselves made of stone and adobe. For the Indigenous people they built wooden huts, hundreds of yards from the church, with roofs of grass and reeds. Uprisings of the newly destitute were held off by soldiers living nearby. Monks always baptized tribes before the soldiers massacred them. The number of Coast Miwok peoples and the more than one hundred languages they spoke declined as the years passed and New Spain became Mexico in the early nineteenth century, American settlers came to outnumber both the Indigenous and the Mexican populations, monks were replaced with friars, and vast tracts of land known as *ranchos* were privatized and gifted to the local Spanish and later Mexican rulers. One of those grants, established just north of Yerba Buena in 1835, was Rancho Sausalito. Less than sixty years later, Sausalito was incorporated and the first city hall was built on a site that was now a fifteen-minute walk along the water from where the city council was gathered.

Toward the end of the meeting, Jeff took to the podium.

"Hello, residents of Sausalito," he started. "People here have come up against this ephemeral issue that is not going to happen. In 2012 it didn't, in 2013 it didn't, in 2014 it didn't. In 2015 chances are it's not going to happen."

He turned to the Hill People, as the anchor-outs referred to wealthy Sausalitans. Maybe everyone could find some common ground: If they didn't want shelters on land, why not allow the anchorage instead?

"We already have room for the homeless out on the water! I'm housing two of them tonight. Okay? I do not want to live in a community where I feel like there is a conflict between the poor and the rich. Jesus said, 'When you give money to the poor who are always with you, do not charge interest.' Okay?"

He turned back to the council members.

"I'm a Jubilee Messenger. I've gone without money basically for a couple of years. I live on a boat. I don't expect everyone to agree with me. At the end of Jubilee, everybody goes back to their ancestral heritage. There is no person without a home." The Jubilee was on its way, only a decade out. Couldn't they find a spot for everyone on the anchorage until the world was made right?

Jeff had been an advocate for unhoused people long before he came to the water in 2000. He had worked at the *Denver Voice*, a paper he described as "for the Mile High homeless." He'd never expected to stay on the water all these years, but as was true of many anchor-outs, he stayed, to some degree, because he was so busy fighting his own eviction.

"Everybody has—not a right, because a right can be taken away. Okay? So now we are in a situation where this issue is not going to happen. They are not going to build a homeless shelter. They are not going to build it anywhere in the near future. That's okay. We can handle it on the water. And I would like each of you in your hearts to look at people as human beings and not as wallets that are empty or rich. I hope somebody comes here and gives a spiritual message. And I hope that next time it doesn't have to be me. I'm not doing this for money. And I hope I'm not doing it for my ego. I pray. So, I'd just like to say: Lokah samastah sukhino bha—"

"Thank you," the mayor interrupted.

"May all beings be happy."

The meeting ended with residents reassured that no shelter would be built.

NONE OF THIS SURPRISED JEFF, OR any of the other anchor-outs. Long ago they'd learned that no space would be made for them on land. Many preferred the water anyway. What they proposed instead was a truce: let the anchorage be the shelter for those without the means to live along the hillside. All the city had to do, with regard to the anchorage, was nothing. Stop the ticketing and the arrests, the seizing of boats and the crushing of homes. *Lokah samastah sukhino bhavantu.*

"The USA has always wavered between hating or loving its steel and rubber tramps—hoboes and hitchhikers, gold rushers, landless immigrants, Indians and cowboys—as well as the town boozers," Jeff later told me. "By the 1980s, the promises of community mental health centers went the way of public housing—defunded and turned to rubble. The village idiots and holy fools, drunks and proletarian hunks, the broke black sheep, likely as not fleeced of their inheritance by greedy families, were thrown onto the tender mercies of American streets, fields, parks, and waters. It was the mirror of Ethan Allen Hawley's betrayal to his best friend and town drunk Danny in Steinbeck's *Winter of Our Discontent*. Ethan knows that the big money he hands Danny won't be used to get treatment, but will buy enough alcohol to kill him, while Ethan inherits Danny's valuable land."

Sausalito, it appeared, was wavering once more.

Jeff wasn't the only one to notice. In the park, Innate had sounded convinced that life on the water was about to get a lot worse. For him, appeals in meetings would no longer be enough. Prayer was good, but sometimes the ways the Lord worked were a little too mysterious. Holding off the RBRA would need to be done in court.

3

HOPING TO FIND OUT MORE, I MET INNATE AND MELISSA AT GATE 6, ON THE northernmost coast of Sausalito, known as Waldo Point.

Gate 6 was the last remains of an older way on the shore. Dozens of houseboats in various stages of exhaustion were tied together by floating wooden walkways, bundles of electrical and phone wires, and a PVC-pipe plumbing system. Many of the residents had been there for decades, and they allowed the anchor-outs to tie up their boats and kayaks to the dinghy dock.

As the sun was setting, we walked out to Innate's motorboat. On either side of us were flowers growing from wheelbarrows and milk crates. Christmas lights were strung between a stone sculpture of the Virgin Mary and an eagle made from melted cans of beer.

Through an open window, Innate noticed the hairy feet of a man watching the local news at low volume.

He put his finger to his lips. He knew the frustration anchor-outs sometimes felt when strangers passed close by. "People came up to the house and asked, 'How do you take a shit?'" Innate whispered, stepping inside his motorboat. "I'd tell them, 'I scrunch my face and some squeaky fart noises come out. How do you do it?'"

The ride to Innate's barge boat took about five minutes. On the way, he pointed down to the anchorage. He was farther north than most people, he said, "out of the punchbowl." That he would be raided by the Coast Guard up here was to him a bad omen.

His barge was maybe thirty feet long by fifteen feet wide. Wrapped around it was a narrow porch whose stability varied by section. The front, Innate explained as he tied the motorboat to his floating dock, was where he and Melissa grew herbs and tomatoes. It could safely support three guests. In the back, however, the wood planks and banisters had come unmoored from the main structure. I'd have to check that out on my own, he told me. More than one person at a time would send it to the bottom of the bay.

Maybe later, I said.

Melissa announced that she would spend the night on land, at the home of a friend.

Innate warned her that he was cooking his "special spaghetti sauce" that night and she wouldn't want to miss it.

Melissa said she'd have leftovers.

He didn't foresee there being leftovers.

She'd take her chances, she told him as she climbed inside a kayak and set out across the water.

The boat's walls and roof were well shingled and watertight, but inside, its floor had become warped over time. I sat down at a plywood table in the center of the room as Innate went to work in the kitchen. He pulled a bag from the foam cooler set into the floor and began slicing vegetables beside his hot plate.

Life was not always this luxurious, he said. When he arrived a decade earlier, he lived on an old sailboat. "But she got drug across the bay in a storm and got caught on a pylon and tangled up in my friend's line." Eventually, he made his way to this boat after his friend Larry inherited another boat from an anchor-out named Shel, who passed away. "Larry lives in Shel's boat, but it's 'Shel's boat.' I live in Larry's boat, but it's 'Larry's boat.'"

This naming tradition, Innate said as he stirred his pot, was one way anchor-outs preserved their history. To watch a boat get seized and crushed was devastating. "Who knows what that little boat has seen. It's like what they are doing in Egypt, driving over monuments with tractors." He was misremembering a news report from Iraq a month earlier. The ruins of the two-thousand-year-old caravan city of Hatra had been destroyed. A semiautonomous territory at the western edge of the Parthian Empire, Hatra had been a center of trade and worship and was governed by princes.

Saying he needed some ingredients that were growing outside in his dirt buckets, Innate disappeared through the doorway.

I looked around the boat. Next to the entrance was the desk over which he'd hung photos of naked women and old movie stars. Trailing from his computer was a nest of wires leading up to the ceiling. Innate and Melissa's bed was pushed against the southern wall. Above it was a bay window through which the lights of San Francisco glowed at night. The toilet was built into a small alcove off the eastern wall, beside an iron heating stove on which a potted flower barely grew.

What was in this sauce? I asked Innate as he threw open the door.

"Mushrooms," he told me. Beyond that he wouldn't say; it was a family secret, passed down to him from his mother.

He pulled a couple of plates from a high shelf and heaped pasta onto them. He set a plate down in front of me and applied spoonful after spoonful of thick purplish sauce.

This was the largest plate of spaghetti I'd ever seen, I told him.

"The sauce is really good, brother," he said, applying more.

And it was: spicy, sweet, floral, like none I'd had before.

A KNOCK CAME AT THE DOOR as we finished our plates.

Innate jumped to attention.

"It's Keven!" a voice shouted.

"Oh hey, brother!"

Keven was wearing crisp blue jeans and white tennis shoes. He had been living on the water for seven years. When he first arrived, he'd planned a brief stay in Richardson Bay, but he was offended when the harbormaster told him he could remain there for only seventy-two hours. Richardson Bay, it seemed, was being run by small-town tyrants. Keven refused to leave. Whatever he'd been searching for on his voyage, he'd found it in this fight. "If they would have never talked to me," he said, "I would have been gone in fourteen days."

Keven handed Innate a paper bag of groceries and sat down at the table.

Innate asked him if he wanted any dinner.

He eyed the purple swirls on my plate. "No," he said.

It's really good, I assured him.

He wasn't here to eat, he said to me as he tossed a sack on the table. He pulled from it dog-eared maps and aerial photos of Richardson Bay. They'd all noticed the uptick in boat seizures, but something wasn't adding up, he told us. Looking at the number of boats in the water over time, he pointed out that it wasn't decreasing. Someone was bringing them in just as quickly as they were taking them out.

Why would they do that?

All kinds of strange things happen out here, said Keven. Maybe somebody gets paid to wreck out these boats after they are taken from the anchor-outs.

So what did he think was going on?

Hard to say. But if someone *was* getting rich, the best way to go unnoticed would be to keep bringing in more vessels.

Innate switched on a lamp. In the soft orange light he eyed Keven's maps, uncertain of this new theory. Sausalito was one of the largest funders of the RBRA. Surely they'd notice if all that money was going to waste?

Keven shrugged and shoved the papers into his bag. The hour was late, and he wanted to get back to his boat.

After he left, I asked Innate what he made of the theory.

Anything *could* be true, he explained. So many theories about the Hill People floated around the anchorage that he didn't have time to vet them all. Luckily, they boiled down to the same problem: the RBRA seizing boats. And for that, he might have found a solution.

He reached for his own stack of printouts on his desk.

Maritime law, he told me, dictates that local authorities can impound a boat only if it is deemed a *vessel*, which US Code defines as any "watercraft or other artificial contrivance used, or capable of being used, as a means of transportation on water." Those authorities, including the RBRA, had long categorized as a vessel just about anything that floated, and that position had held up well in court. In 1982, the Fifth Circuit Court of Appeals, for example, stated that "one probably could make a convincing case for Jonah inside the whale" being a vessel. However, in a case Innate had recently come across, the city of Riviera Beach, Florida, after an unsuccessful attempt to evict a houseboat from its waters, convinced the district court to order the home put up for public auction. The city then bought it and crushed it. The owner fought back and sued, taking the case all the way to the US Supreme Court, which found that a stationary houseboat was not necessarily a vessel, and thus not subject to a city's admiralty jurisdiction. "To state the obvious," wrote Justice Stephen Breyer in 2013, "a wooden washtub, a plastic dishpan, a swimming platform on pontoons, a large fishing net, a door taken off its hinges, or Pinocchio (when inside the whale) are not 'vessels.'"

Into the night, Innate made the case that many of the boats crushed by the RBRA would fit Breyer's non-vessel criteria. The anchor-outs would flood the city with lawsuits.

Finally, realizing the time, Innate packed the leftover pasta into the floor cooler and crawled under the mound of quilts on his bed. There was no sleeping late on the water, he warned. Something always saw to that.

I curled up on two cushions behind the table.

As I drifted off to sleep, I recalled a story Innate had told me in Dunphy Park. He'd gone into a Burger King and asked the clerk for a tub of barbecue sauce, only to discover that it would cost him twenty cents. "She's protecting against me coming in every day, taking five sauces, and selling them outside," he said. That's the way it was on the hill: everyone assumed the worst of one another. But the anchor-outs didn't want to take and take. They just needed a free tub of dipping sauce now and then.

That night, more than once, I awoke to the whispers of strangers rowing by the door.

THE NEXT MORNING, INNATE ROSE TO his usual routine.

He sat up in bed, coughed a bit, and pulled back the curtain to see who might be floating past. The seal that had been coming around lately was already barking at him.

Nnnnate, nnnnate, nnnnate!

The light on the water was orange, so it must have been around 7:00 a.m. He put his feet on the floor, coughed a few more times, and made for the shelves by the water basin on the other side of the room. He picked up a can of tuna and walked out onto the floating dock.

The seal was waiting near a sun-bleached kayak, still barking.

"I can't help but think he's an anchor-out," Innate told me as he scraped the tuna into the bay with his finger. The seal snatched up the bits of fish and began rolling its body against the kayak's wet plastic hull. "Maybe he thinks it's another seal. Or maybe he is tired and just wants to get out of the water."

The night's chill had yet to lift. Only a few anchor-outs were in their dinghies. Innate watched as the two gulls that nested on his roof landed in his bucket garden. The male bird limped. One of his feet was mangled with old damage, like a city pigeon's. Innate had taken to calling him Goofy; the other he called Broad, "because she's Goofy's Broad." He opened another can of tuna and set it out on an overturned bucket.

The birds ate, and the wake of a passing boat rolled through.

Back inside, two of the Siamese cats that lived in the rafters were circling an empty casserole dish. Both of them, Tom and Lucy, had belonged to Larry. They had lived in the boat longer than Innate had; Tom's former partner, Rosie, had been there even longer, since the 1990s. It is believed that she fell into the water and drowned, but all that was known for certain was that Rosie hadn't been seen in years.

Innate removed the bowl of leftover spaghetti from a cooler and scooped its contents into the casserole dish. Spooky, a six-toed Siamese, jumped down from the rafters and joined his parents for breakfast.

The percolator on the hot plate began to boil.

Innate poured himself a cup of coffee and sat down at the table. In the early light, I noticed that the surface was littered with ashtrays and a few books on the history and geography of Sausalito. Innate pinched some tobacco from a Tupperware container and rolled a cigarette. He opened up his guide to Northern California tides and planned the morning.

We could take it slow. The water would be above the sandbar for a while yet. Maybe he'd power up the laptop. Occasionally, he said, he devoted a few hours of battery life to playing *Grand Theft Auto Five* while listening to "Ave Maria."

Tom and Lucy began hissing in the rafters above us.

Innate laughed.

As a kid, I asked Innate, did he ever imagine a life like this?

In some ways, he said, he had always been moving in this direction. He was born in San Diego in 1968, a second-born twin. His brother, who was stillborn, was given the name "No. 1" on his birth certificate, the same legal name as his father, who had a twin brother named "No. 2." Innate and his five siblings all lived for a while in a mansion in the suburbs. No. 1 had done well by the family, operating a beauty salon in a hotel plaza downtown. As a young kid in his father's shop, Innate pretended that the chairs with hair-drying helmets were rocket ships and he earned fifty-cent pieces for sweeping up hair clippings.

Did he still talk to his father?

Innate shook his head. His father had disappeared when he was five. It was only much later in his life that he would learn what became of the old man: one day, No. 1 gave up his beauty shop, discarded all of his possessions aside from a backpack and a walking stick, and journeyed to Laguna Beach, where he spent the next few decades sweeping sidewalks. By the time No. 1 died in 2010, he had taken to pronouncing his name as *No One*. "What happened was, he was engrossed in the capability of what money can produce, then came to realize the wrongness of that. He, I believe, wanted to get away from the requirements—responsibilities—of that life."

Not long after his father left, his two oldest brothers, including Richard, who would later go by Dream Weaver, ran away from home. His mother began collecting food stamps and moved the family to a farm owned by her new husband, an electrician named Ken. Innate's sister and mother spent their days inside, scrubbing the floors and cooking meals. He and his brother repaired fences and tended to the animals, castrating or slaughtering the cows, depending on the season. Ken taught them to "let nature work." They planted corn before a big rain to save themselves from having to water the crops; and they tossed poisonous snakes down gopher holes to kill the rodents. He learned how to churn butter and skin foxes, and how to wire batteries and drain fields.

Innate spent his childhood believing that his stepfather was a harsh and rigid man. He dropped out of high school and moved into the trailer of his friend's family. He married young and had two sons. But after a back injury, the life he was building began to unravel. He got divorced and began using and growing medical marijuana, leading to his arrest in 2006. Once he was released, he decided to leave San Diego. He packed his dog and everything he owned into a U-Haul and headed north, toward no place in particular. He stopped at a diner in nearby Rainbow, a small mountain town in northern San Diego County. While he was inside, someone stole his U-Haul, and with it his dog. "I just started thinking, everything I owned just burned in a fire," he said.

Dream Weaver was already living on the anchorage. With nowhere else to go, Innate decided to join his brother. He bought a seat on a Greyhound bus and headed north to Richardson Bay.

I asked Innate if Sausalito gave him trouble at first.

No, he said. It was calmer at that time.

What caused things to change?

Maybe fear, he guessed, driven by the anchorage doubling in size. The anchor-outs didn't own land or have big pastel-colored mansions. Nothing that marked one's station in life onshore mattered out on the water. "It's like an old children's story," he told me. "There's a walrus standing at the edge of an icy shoreline and a puffin pops up and says, 'What are you looking at?' and the walrus says, 'That spot.' The puffin says, 'What spot?' and the walrus says, 'That spot, in the snow.' And the walrus notices a tiny black spot in the snow. So they start guessing what it is. The puffin says, 'I know, it's the tip of a bird's wing.' The walrus says, 'No, it's the mast of a ship.' So they dig around the spot, and they find this thing, and they don't know what it is. You and I would know it is a wagon. But they don't know what the fuck it is because they live in the snow. Soon the snow gets blown onto the hole and the puffin gets buried. The walrus digs him up. But the puffin almost died. So they push the wagon out to sea. Then a polar bear comes along and sees it on the horizon and says, 'What's that out there? That spot?' And the puffin and the walrus say, 'What spot? It's nothing.' And that's the end of the story."

He pulled from his cigarette and pointed at me.

"But it's the beginning of the mindset of fear," he said, blowing smoke into the sunbeam between us.

He donned his bathrobe and bowler hat and hustled me onto the dock.

We took in the fresh bay air.

Across the estuary, anchor-outs were packing their dinghies and heading for shore. Some would ride their bikes out to the suburbs, to lay bricks or frame homes for local contractors. Others would trade their valuables or labor to a neighbor for a can of coffee or a spare line.

Trade had long been the way of the estuary. Before the Gold Rush, goods were often preferred over cash. Goods were harder to tax and steal. Locals exchanged what they called "California bank notes"—animal hides backed by the fur market in Boston. Three hides might fetch fifty pounds of whale tallow, all but guaranteed by the demand for oil in South America. There was even a time in the late 1850s, after a fire burned down much of San Francisco, that New York banks stopped taking currency issued in California altogether.

Innate surveyed the water. There was no sign of the harbormaster.

It wasn't that everyone in Sausalito was evil, he told me as he loaded his gear into the motorboat. It was just that the world crushed the people not built for it, and those people needed places like the anchorage. Sausalitans forgot that from time to time.

Back in the 1970s, all of Waldo Point looked like Gate 6. Hundreds lived in floating shacks made of wood and scrap metal that they salvaged from the Marinship Yard after World War II. Some had come from Haight-Ashbury. Others just drifted in off the back roads of Northern California. There were addicts, artists, and veterans all living together along the water. But in time the Hill People lost patience. Views from their homes were ruined, they said. They complained that the houseboats lacked a sewer system, overlooking the fact that their own wastewater treatment plant pumped refuse into Richardson Bay. Eventually, authorities condemned, arrested, and bulldozed much of the community into oblivion.

There were still a few guys around who remembered the House-boat Wars, as the whole affair became known. Larry, who was in his nineties now, had been there for all of it. He knew the Hill People were capable of turning on the waterfront denizens. He knew how bad it could get.

Get in, Innate said. He'd take me to Larry. I should hear it from him.

He pulled the starter cord and the old motor shook to life.

4

"THIS IS SHEL'S BOAT," INNATE SAID AS I TRAILED HIM UP THE RAMP OF the two-story balloon barge. Officially named the *Evil Eye*, the craft had been designed by Shel a half-century earlier. Built atop it, as if from a children's story, was a wooden cabin.

The door was cracked open.

"He's home," Innate told me as he pushed his way inside.

It was dark but for the green and red beams of stained-glass light casting the shadows of ancient electronics. Cats shifted their positions among plants as we walked to the back room.

Larry was seated on a deck chair, shirtless, drinking from a goblet of water. Next to him was an oxygen tank. He twisted his long white beard as he watched, unmoved, while his Siamese cats Leroy, Mumbo, Jumbo, and Handsome Harry followed me inside.

I sat down at a table, careful not to tip the stacks of unopened mail. Along the walls were fallen frames housing familiar black-and-white line drawings. At once it occurred to me that "Shel" was the author Shel Silverstein, who died in 1999.

"What do you do?" asked Larry, drumming his long fingernails on a book of Karl Marx quotations.

I told him I was a reporter—

"But he's okay," Innate interrupted. "He's not looking for a scoop."

Innate turned his attention to a library of videocassettes mounted on the wall. There looked to be a hundred tapes, each one labeled by subject. There was "Sunrise," "Dry Hump," "Fish Head Tom," and "Fish Head Tom Sinking."

"You know, I had a big scoop once," said Larry. In the 1950s, he was a photographer for the Associated Press. "I was in Moscow, eating at a Chinese restaurant—probably the only Chinese restaurant in Moscow. And I start going back and forth with these two Chinese guys, big guys, about Marxism or something. And they asked me if I wanted to meet their guys in China. And so I said, 'Sure.' It turns out they were government officials. And I was the first journalist to meet Mao. I'm not trying to brag about that, it's just that we were talking about scoops."

It sounded almost unbelievable, I said.

"That really happened!" He told me it was on that trip in 1957 that he first met Shel. "Shel was doing a story for *Playboy*. I had just gone in to see Lenin and Stalin. Lenin is still there. Stalin was there too. They had just found out what a crazy motherfucker he was. I wanted to see what they looked like. Lenin looked tired. Stalin looked better than most of the people looking at him."

Larry ended up working as the photographer for Shel's *Playboy* column. In 1967, the magazine sent them to Haight-Ashbury in San Francisco. They stayed for three months—until "the Summer of Love," Larry said, "turned to the Winter of Our Discontent"— and then moved across the Golden Gate to join the houseboaters in Waldo Point. "I got here, and I said: 'I don't ever want to do anything again for the rest of my life.'"

IN THE TIME BEFORE LARRY AND Shel arrived, the waterfront dwellers were a mix of laborers, fishermen, sailors, and even a few city workers. They were rough and committed people. Though no one had much money, they all minded their own business. And their landlord, a shipyard owner named Don Arques, minded his too.

The Arques family had a long history in Richardson Bay. In the years after the Earthquake and Fire of 1906, Don's father, a Portuguese shipbuilder named Camillo, made wooden boats along the shore. During World War I, the US Navy contracted with him to manufacture hauling vessels. By the 1930s, he was partnered with Don, and the pair set out to grow the operation: they towed to shore abandoned arc-boats from the nineteenth century; they purchased passenger ferries like the *Charles Van Damme* and the *San Rafael*, which had each been decommissioned after the Golden Gate Bridge was completed; and following World War II, they bought up the Navy's surplus barges, along with much of the Marinship Yard itself.

Arques eventually acquired what became known as Bob's Boatyard, a muddy stretch of coastline that had hosted shipbuilders for half a century. In the 1870s, the town's few residents repaired fishing vessels there. By the 1880s, schooners, much like the *Galilee* itself, were being produced at the Atlantic Boat Building Works and later, during World War I, at the Oceanic Boatyard, which replaced it.

Sausalito's waterfront real estate became some of the most prized in California. But Arques, who lived on a cattle ranch, never saw a reason to sell. Nor to develop. Anyone who pleased came and went in Richardson Bay, often to the city's dismay.

Arques disdained authority. The story was well known on the waterfront of a time when police officers issued him a ticket for parking in front of a fire hydrant. Every day afterward, he parked in front of the same hydrant, and more and more tickets accrued, until the city impounded his car. Still, he did nothing. The tires rotted, the door rusted. When it was unsalvageable, he finally went to court and contested the fines. Unbeknownst to the police, the tickets were invalid because Arques owned the hydrant. A judge forced the city to buy him a brand-new car.

Likewise, he treated with contempt the city's concerns about the squatters on his land, though privately he shared many of its grievances. He let soldiers returning from World War II and later Vietnam build dwellings in Gates 3, 5, and 6. Artists and fishermen joined them. Abandoned military barges and balloon boats were converted into homes, among them the *Evil Eye*. Arques ostensibly charged rent, but many never paid. City officials referred to him as the "Howard Hughes of Sausalito": he owned everything but was impossible to reach. When questioned about the squatters by the *Wall Street Journal*, Arques replied: "I don't pay any attention to them."

As the sixties wore on, however, a new crowd began moving in from San Francisco. They were mostly white, in their twenties and thirties, with middle-class parents to whom they could return. With them they brought their difficulties: addiction, burnout, desperation. They shot out streetlights and built shacks, called "shooting galleries," where they used heroin together. An employee of Arques's recorded the drowning deaths of at least three children while their parents were at the galleries. Meanwhile, four murders, six suicides, and countless overdose deaths on the waterfront made addressing the situation feel to many Sausalitans like a moral imperative.

City officials fixated, however, on pollution. Waste, human and otherwise, was going into the bay, a problem guaranteed by Marin County's refusal to let the squatters hook up to the district sewer line. They responded by pushing one another to adopt chemical toilets, for which they ran a campaign in *Fresh Garlic*, their self-published community newspaper. The initiative worked, but not for long. The city next began to complain of trash in the boatyard. Arques in turn purchased a garbage truck, but the victory was again short-lived. By the 1970s, it was clear that the city, the county, and the BCDC were intent on clearing and redeveloping the land.

When officials posted condemnation notices on shacks and boats, the squatters fought back, often violently. They held midnight meetings on the *Charles Van Damme* and hatched their plans to stand firm against the police and the bulldozers and fill-trucks sent to destroy them. The end came when the city mobilized its boat crusher, nicknamed the *Clamshell*. According to *Fresh Garlic*, it demolished homes at ten times the cost of relocating them.

The waterfront was transformed. Some residents, like Shel, purchased or won berths on the new docks. Others, Larry among them, drifted out to the anchorage. By 1979, one local newsletter was referring to a stretch of waterfront as "Millionaires Row." According to a contributor, it had been taken over by "a sea captain, four captains of industry, ten would be captains of industry, [and] some of the usual variety of Marin affluence makers."

Arques died a decade later, in 1993, by which point much of the coast had been bought up by private developers. A new houseboat in Sausalito could fetch over $1 million.

LARRY SMILED AT HANDSOME HARRY, WHO was lapping milk from a dish by my feet.

Life out here sounded harsh, I told him.

He shook his head. Life was harsh everywhere. But back then, despite all the violence and fighting, it was paradise. Allen Ginsberg and Alan Watts showed up from time to time. Jean Varda lived for a while on the decommissioned *Vallejo*. And there were dry docks in the bay where they all sang and danced together, until the night when the city paid a man fifty dollars to burn it all down.

I looked over at Innate, still sitting by the video library. He was holding a cassette that Larry had shot years ago labeled "Dry Hump."

"The No Name Bar—now that's a story!" Larry shouted.

Innate clarified that the bar was a place along Bridgeway where anchor-outs and Hill People used to drink together.

"There was a time, maybe not anymore, when the No Name Bar was the greatest bar in the entire world. It had the best graffiti on the walls. On a lonely night, I would go there and see an old girlfriend, and she'd take me into the men's room, and while she was giving me a blow job I'd be writing down the graffiti on the wall. It was just that kind of place."

Was the No Name still operating?

It was, said Innate. But the clientele had changed.

Then I noticed the time. I had a ferry to catch.

"Ah, a disciplined man," Larry said. "We don't get many of those out here." Upon my exit, he shouted: "Just write a good story. I don't care if it's true."

THE FERRY LANDING WAS IN DOWNTOWN Sausalito, a few miles south of the *Evil Eye*'s berth on Liberty Dock.

I walked along Bridgeway, a two-lane boulevard that runs the length of Sausalito, separating the hill from the waterfront. In the nineteenth century, the corridor was the path of the North Pacific Coast Railroad's line connecting the Bay Area to the lumber-rich north. Called Water Street until the construction of the Golden Gate Bridge in the 1930s, Bridgeway was regularly clogged with cars in line to board ferries to San Francisco.

I ran into Bo beneath the shade of a tree in Dunphy Park. He was adjusting the chain on his bicycle, which he'd painted gold.

I just passed two of your paintings, I said. They were in the bushes in front of the gas station.

He perked up.

One was a finger painting of the San Francisco skyline. Another was of the anchorage.

"You can have one," he said. "Bring it back and I'll sign it."

I retrieved the cityscape and returned with a ten-dollar bill.

Bo fished a straw and a tube of paint from his bucket and went to work on the corner of the painting.

"There you go!" He'd signed it "*VanBo*," written upside down.

After we parted, I waited for the next ferry at the No Name Bar. The inside was dark and narrow, with a sunlit patio in back. Save for me, the bartender, and a waitress, it was empty.

How did the name originate? I asked.

"They bought the bar from some other dude, and they couldn't figure out a name," the bartender said. "Now it's fifty-six years later."

I told them what Larry remembered of the No Name Bar.

"Larry!" shouted the waitress. She'd been there since the seventies. "There was never any graffiti on the walls."

A MONTH LATER, I STOPPED BY the No Name Bar on my way to the park. The bartender, I hoped, would direct me to some people on the hill who might remember the Houseboat Wars of Larry's day.

"I know who you are," he laughed when I greeted him.

Could he think of anyone in town who'd talk to me?

"No," he said.

What about someone who'd share their thoughts on the anchor-outs?

"I don't know how many ways I can tell you no!"

Apologizing, I left.

The bartender's response was familiar. Locals were not always eager to share their opinions on the anchor-outs. Many were sympathetic: they knew how expensive Sausalito was, how hard the last seven years had been on a lot of people. In the past, they had never wanted to see anyone evicted from the water. But it appeared, at least to them, that many of the new arrivals had no ability to keep their boats afloat and had come in desperation, bringing along their struggles with drug and alcohol abuse and the violence those addictions beget. Somebody had to do something. But what the solution was, they couldn't say.

At the park, I spotted Rose, a single mother who lived on a boat just offshore.

She was in her early twenties, she told me, and had moved to the anchorage from Washington State only six months earlier. "I came for the opportunities," she said.

She knelt down in the grass to play with her toddler, but the child ran off.

The father was from a previous relationship. "My mom is staying with my ex-boyfriend," she said. "My ex's mom kicked him out, so he called my mom for some reason. My family should be on *Jerry Springer*."

Rose had been receiving disability benefits since she arrived. "But it's not enough. So I'm trying to become famous—it's the only way." She pulled out her flip phone and read me a list of puns she had written for a comedy act:

> *Tunafish? I can't even tune a piano!*
> *Seareously the best joke ever.*
> *I'm not even squidding.*
> *If you can think of a better fish pun let minnow.*
> *I didn't do it on porpoise.*
> *I've been delta bad hand.*

"I'm pretty funny. I can also fake-cry, stick my fist in my mouth, and I once won a staring contest with an iguana."

Rose laughed and looked off at something in the distance, until a big gray pigeon in a nearby gravel lot captured her attention. His breast was puffed out, and he was chasing a female. "They try to have sex," she said, shaking her head. She kicked rocks at the male bird. "Leave her alone!" The pigeons flew away. "I have these birds fucking on my boat. It's annoying. I have a kid."

I glanced out across the park, looking for her daughter, whom I spotted by a gazebo, next to a young boy blowing carelessly into a harmonica.

Rose had hoped that living on the anchorage would allow her to develop her stand-up act in San Francisco. But she managed to make the trip only once a month, to receive treatment for her multiple sclerosis. Travel was costly, and her only income, aside from her benefits, came from selling local coffee shop customers roses dipped in wax.

Still, she was optimistic. Some anchor-outs had told her of an alternative MS treatment: roasted dandelions. "We mix them with tea or food, and we cook them, put them in the oven on low," she said.

Did it work?

"I don't know," she said. But she'd just moved onto a new boat, and it had the perfect barrel on the deck in which she could plant flowers.

Where did you live before the move? I asked.

Her first home, known as the *Projectile*, was a long black barge that seemed to invite misfortune. "Some guy got stabbed on it," she said. "It's just a bunch of crazy shit in this nice town."

Maybe the rough old waterfront of Larry's day had never left?

She pointed to a spot along the shoreline of the park, where several kayaks and dinghies were tied up, jostling one another as the breeze blew in. The previous week, she told me, she'd found a dead body there. "It was eight in the morning, before I dropped my daughter off at school. He was floating right there by that white boat."

She pulled out her phone again. "I took a picture," she said, showing me a black-and-white photo of an older man floating face up. His shirt was open. "It looked like the life was sucked out of him. They shut the whole park down. They don't know what happened."

Rose didn't say much else about the man. One of the only news stories published about his death ran at about 150 words in the *Marin Independent Journal*. It said that there were signs of injuries, but gave no indication as to how he died.

"People think someone out here did it," Rose said.

Just then, Rose's daughter wandered back over and grabbed a clementine from a mesh bag resting against a fence post.

"Give some to the birds," her mother told her.

After the pigeons had gotten their fill, Rose shooed them away once more.

LATER THAT DAY, I WALKED UP the shore to the *Evil Eye*, to ask Larry about the body Rose found.

As I stepped inside, I called out to Larry and his wife, Diane, but no one responded.

I found Larry sitting next to his oxygen tank in the bedroom. It was stuffy and dark, gloomier than usual. A light was flashing from an opening in the floor that led belowdecks, where Diane was watching *The Queen of Versailles* on a small television. Larry looked tired, and it occurred to me that much of his life was now spent in that chair.

I sat down at the table, where Handsome Harry was lapping up a mug of water next to a joint burning in an ashtray.

"We used to have raccoons come in all the time," Larry said. "I figured I'd let them eat, but big Harry chased them all out. He's a bad motherfucker. Thing is, it's kind of dumb to fuck with a raccoon."

I asked Larry about why so little was known of the dead man.

He paused. Larry didn't say whether he knew him, though he nodded to indicate that he understood the question. Instead, he began telling me about working at the Pearl Harbor Naval Shipyard in the days after the base was attacked. One of his jobs, he explained, was to cut holes in the capsized hull of the *Oklahoma*. "We got them out, but they were all dead. Kids—eighteen, nineteen, twenty. My great lesson about war was, you either end up like this guy or you end up looking down at this guy."

He took a sip of water from his goblet, followed by a hit off the joint.

"You want to be ninety-one? Do a bunch of things they tell

you you shouldn't be doing. You'll get to be a pallbearer for all your doctors."

Smoke swirled from Larry's mouth. He spoke about God. "God was a great character who lived down here. Cuban guy. Said he was God. He threw his harp and his teeth out the window. He made Joe Gould look like a fucking Girl Scout. One day he walked down the dock with a machete, cutting boat lines. Last thing I heard about him, he stole a police car."

I reminded Larry that I'd asked about the dead man.

Larry frowned, like I hadn't been paying attention. "Could be anyone! It was a great nickname place down here. Thunderpussy, Sick Rick, Slick Rick, Normal Norman, Abnormal Norman, Nearly Normal Norman. The only way you found out a guy's real name was after he croaked. God tried to get his name changed legally. He wanted to sign checks as 'God.' The judge wouldn't let him do it. But he let him do 'Ubiquitous God.'"

Larry lowered his voice. "Twelve-String Pete," he said. "He was one of the bad ones. He was dosing babies with PCP. One day he ended up face down in a swimming pool. 'Twelve-String Pete from Down the Street.' That's how he introduced himself. Once in a while some bad actors would come in. We had a few guys, one guy had to go down and talk to them and you'd never see them again. He was our local guy. It would have to be a guy who could do the thing. There are some hard-core people out there. Heavy-duty people. People that have done some shit. A lot of old smugglers, probably some dope dealers. It's not an easy life out there—especially for women."

As we spoke, Diane climbed up through the opening in the floor to greet me. Larry asked her to make him a cup of coffee.

"It will keep you up all night," she said, adding that he would be in a lousy mood tomorrow.

"I don't give a shit."

"I know." She sighed, then descended to the deck below.

Handsome Harry leapt off the table.

"I've been in love with cats for fifty years," Larry said. "They're always part of my scene."

I asked him why he thought that was.

"It's hard to say," he responded. "If a cat picks you, it's a totally different thing than when you pick them. It's a whole other ball game. They've been doing this shit for thousands of years. And when it's cold out on the boat, there is a certain point where you're sleeping with a cat. There is something about it that your consciousness and their consciousness meet."

Larry paused and seemed to reconsider his answer. "Why do you love anything? A friend of mine calls me the other day and asks, 'Do you love your wife?' I thought, 'Wow, what a question.' I had to think about that. I meant to ask him why he asked me that. I'll have to ask him, or maybe not. There are some things you don't ask about."

5

OVER THE MONTHS I'D GOTTEN TO KNOW THEM, THE ANCHOR-OUTS DE-
scribed their world in all different ways: "society gumbo," a "wash-
ing machine," the "war zone." And they linked their story to the
Coast Miwok people, the Alta California fishermen, and the gold
rushers of San Francisco.

Of late, I'd begun to wonder about that last connection, that
of anchor-outs to argonauts: Why did they so frequently draw it,
given that many of them, like the dead man in the park, found only
misfortune?

Upon my return home, I learned that their history was more
intertwined with the gold rushers than I'd imagined.

The Gold Rush began in the 1840s, when the treasure that the
Spaniards had long ago sought was struck at the mines of San Fer-
nando. Hearing reports of gold and the mercury needed to extract
it, the US consul in Alta California alerted the secretary of state that
he had "no doubt" the region was rich in the precious metal, along
with silver, copper, quicksilver, lead sulfur, and coal; he was also
"very certain" that the Mexican government was close to discover-
ing it. Within days, American soldiers marched into Mexico, pushed
the Mexican army south of the Rio Grande, and declared war. Two
years later, on the Fourth of July in 1848, the Treaty of Guadalupe
Hidalgo was announced and Mexico ceded its landholdings north
of the Rio Grande. After the United States took possession of Alta
California, President James K. Polk announced that the metal had
been found.

Stories of the gold traveled to Utah and across the Louisiana Purchase territory. They spread south and west, to Peru and Chile, to China and Australia. Desperate men boarded ships and made the miserable passage across the Pacific, or from Europe and Africa around Cape Horn, trading cholera and diphtheria with one another as they shared their hopes for finding fortune. By 1851, argonauts had arrived from so many places that the English shilling, the American quarter dollar, the French franc, and the Mexican double-real were all exchanged for one another in San Francisco. Soon there would be Indian rupees, Dutch florins, and German guilders in the mix. By one account, every currency in Europe and South America was circulated during the Gold Rush.

The bay filled up with boats abandoned by the new arrivals— over three hundred in 1849, and double that number by the next year. Many were dragged up on the mudflats to serve as warehouses and lodgings, as saloons, churches, and hotels. In short order, the city took shape. Steam shovels pushed sandy hills into the water. Roads were planked over with wood and lined with streetlights. The first electric telegraph line was strung. Newspapers were founded, including one, in Monterey, called *The California*, which lacked the ability to print the letter *w* because it was printed on a Spanish-made press. "In due time vve vvill do better," wrote the publisher.

As fortunes blossomed, the city's newly rich moved into the hills, only returning to the flats on weekends to visit the theater or to watch bears and bulls fight one another to the death in the Mission District. These were the men who'd found gold early on, panning rivers and extracting the metal near the earth's surface. They built the grand Victorian mansions in Sausalito and then parceled up the land, established a stock exchange, and invested in ferry and railroad companies.

For those argonauts who came later, San Francisco was a miserable place. Gold was harder and harder to find. The city had become increasingly male and drunk, and with a homicide rate more than twenty times what it is today, the police force could do little but record the causes of death: "quarrel," "poison," "gambling dispute," "bound floater," "headless floater." Eventually, a brig named the *Euphemia* was anchored on the shore and converted to a city prison, replacing the Old Calaboose, a jail so flimsy that inmates were known to break the door off and show up at the office of the alcalde to remind him to serve breakfast.

The jails, alleys, and abandoned boats filled up with people who, as one 1850 account put it, had "miscalculated" the "nature of the country" but had no hope of affording safe passage back home.

Reading of the fate of most of the argonauts, I was reminded of the anchor-outs and the way they spoke of the United States: a place where anything could happen but where good things rarely did.

When I'd first met Innate, not long after his fight with the Coast Guard, he offered his theory of why that was. A century ago, a "secret society" of judges, generals, justices, and politicians had conspired to "abate the Constitution" by taking the country off the gold standard so they could print as much currency for themselves as they pleased. The New Deal, by his reckoning, was the bribe they'd offered the poor and working-class public to go along. Or as Bo put it, the guys on top were thieves.

Two months later, in June, Innate completed his documentary about the anchorage and sent me a copy. Toward the end was a video of him in a dark boat cabin, reading a speech delivered in 1944 by the federal judge Learned Hand:

> What is this liberty which must lie in the hearts of men and women? It is not the ruthless, the unbridled will; it is not freedom to do as one likes. That is the denial of liberty, and leads straight to its overthrow. A society in which men recognize no check upon their freedom soon becomes a

society where freedom is the possession of only a savage few;
as we have learned to our sorrow.

Following his speech was footage of anchor-outs swinging from
ship masts, tracked to Nina Simone singing "I Wish I Knew How It
Would Feel to Be Free."

ON THE FOURTH OF JULY, BO and Dream were in the park.

They were in a good mood. For the occasion, some Sausalitans
had set out a spread of casserole trays on folding tables. Bo filled an
egg carton with rice, while Dream scooped meat into a plastic cherry
crate.

What did they think of the Fourth? I asked.

"It's just after the third and before the fifth," Dream told me.
The holiday, like the country itself, had gotten off track.

What do you mean? I asked.

He laughed. Did I really not know that the Continental Congress declared independence from Great Britain on July 2, 1776?

Just then, Rose joined the line behind them. "Here's some
plates," she said, attempting to hand Dream some paperware.

He waved her away as rice fell through the holes of his container,
much to his dog's delight.

Dream told me that he and Innate had a brother, Simple Matters, who also lived on the water but was off in Maine, visiting his
son who'd been sentenced to a decade in prison for elevated aggra-
vated assault. Simple, he told me, was writing a seven-volume novel,
The Gift of the Priceless Pearl, that was dedicated to the victim and
to his son's "free breaths." The book appeared to be based in part on
the Gospel of Mary, a gnostic text, often thought to refer to Mary
Magdalene, in which Jesus tells Peter: "That's why you get sick and
die, because you love what tricks you."

Dream picked up a raw egg from the table.

"He stabbed a guy twenty-one times," he said, dropping the egg gently into the breast pocket of his flannel.

I noticed a nearby pile of clementines. On the anchorage they were as common as cigarettes. I asked Dream where they came from.

"A lady brings them," he said. "I don't know who, and I don't really care. Her son lives offshore. It doesn't mean she will continue to do it, just that she has been doing it—and it's all good."

While they ate, I walked over by the shoreline, where the grass turned to sand. A nineteen-year-old with blond dreadlocks was off on his own, pacing in and out of the water.

He was in trouble, he told me. His girlfriend was pregnant, but he had no job, no means to support her. This, he figured, was the end of the line. His eyes were pink from crying, and his pant legs were soaked to the knees.

What do you think you will do? I asked.

He looked out at the estuary. Maybe he'd bail and move out onto the water, he said, if the anchor-outs would give him a boat.

I didn't respond, though I imagined they would.

I spent much of that afternoon a few blocks up the hill from the park at a bar called Smitty's. The building sat on the original site of the hacienda of William Richardson, the sea captain for whom the bay was named. Later, it housed a bottling plant, which was bought by a former railroad man named Smitty, who turned it into a bar and then won the lottery and sold it to his daughter.

On a bench outside the door, a man was smoking a cigarette.

I told him I was visiting the anchorage.

"It's a problem," he said. "Crime and robberies onshore and off have gone up." He took another drag of his cigarette. "It's a shame. They've been there a long time."

Inside, the room was big and airy, though it still smelled like stale smoke. At the bar was a group of locals in polos and khaki shorts. They were killing time until the fireworks, they told me.

Before long, the anchor-outs came up in the conversation, as they often do in Smitty's.

A man leaned over to me, as if to share a secret. "When you are talking about the anchor-outs, you are talking about homeless people," he said. "People who live under a bridge in LA."

What was his point? I asked.

He shrugged and leaned away.

A woman slung her arm around the man's shoulder and shouted to the bar. "We need a ride over to the yacht club. Anyone going that way?"

A group obliged the woman, and everyone promised to see one another that evening for the fireworks.

After they left, I asked an older man who'd been quietly sipping a beer about the body that washed up in Dunphy Park.

"The guy that got stabbed?"

I told him I wasn't sure: that detail hadn't been reported in the news.

"This is a small town," he said, before leaving for the yacht club as well.

The private club, to which members paid up to $2,500 in annual dues, was close by, only a short walk from where the anchor-outs were eating their rice and eggs.

THE IDEA THAT A CITY OF great wealth needn't be built atop impoverished communities was, for the economist Henry George, an obvious "mirage." By the time the American Industrial Revolution was underway, it had become clear to George that the fates of the two communities were bound together, and though their origins varied by city, the end result always looked the same: "The almshouses and prisons," George wrote in 1879, "are as surely the marks of material progress as are costly dwellings, rich warehouses, and magnificent churches."

In Gold Rush San Francisco, George's observation held true. As mining profits grew for the early arrivals, so too did the liquidity of their banks, whose board members looked to put the cash to work in the great and speculative ventures of the Industrial Revolution: in the railroads that tripled in length as they crept ever westward, connecting Boston to Chicago and at last crossing the Missouri River; in the telegraph wires that were strung along the tracks of the so-called Iron Horse, growing fivefold as they stitched together the newsrooms and trading floors of San Francisco, New York, and, later, London; and in the steel mills cropping up in the Northeast and along the Great Lakes, forging pig iron into the steel demanded for longer, heavier trains to deliver the country's labor force to the urban manufacturing centers, which were increasing in size by almost 60 percent a year.

San Francisco, whose population, at forty-two thousand in 1852, was increasing at ten times the rate of the country as a whole, would face the first test of its new financial institutions in the 1850s. By the middle of the decade, Northern California was already suffering from declining gold production. The city's largest bank, Page, Bacon & Company, which facilitated the shipment of almost one-quarter of all gold out of California, was owned by a parent house in St. Louis that was heavily involved in financing the construction of the Ohio & Mississippi Railway. The railroad's expansion west had relied on funds raised on the bond markets in London and Paris, but that source dried up as Europe's capital was shifted to the Crimean War. In 1855, the St. Louis house became insolvent and failed. When word arrived in San Francisco, Page, Bacon & Company failed as well, prompting a bank run that eventually brought down more than two hundred businesses in the city.

The bust caught up with the rest of the country a year later, when the Treaty of Paris was signed and the fighting in Europe ceased. European agricultural production resumed and demand for US farm products plummeted, causing the Ohio Life Insurance and Trust

Company, which was heavily invested in American agribusiness, to collapse in 1857. When the nation's newly strung telegraph network carried the news to banks and exchanges across the country, panic ensued. Meanwhile, without much gold coming out of California, banks found themselves unable to offer businesses the lines of credit they relied on to maintain their inventory. The production and sale of food and goods fell, and with it demand for railroad services. As rail stocks dropped, it became clear that many banks had poured their customers' savings into high-risk ventures that existed only on paper and whose value had been inflated with lucrative but never-to-be-realized contracts with barons who left only ruin and pending antitrust legislation in their wake.

Hundreds of businesses failed during the Panic of 1857, stranding many young men who had left home on the back of the nation's rail system and headed west in search of gold and wage labor. These luckless prospectors and laid-off workers were the same people who had spent the decade building, sawing, digging, dredging, bay filling, pounding, panning, and hammering fortunes for the city's power brokers. Now, they had become the new and permanent unhoused class. In a decades-old city in a decade-old state, there were no local or federal services to help them. They slept in tent encampments in the hills, squatted on overlooked corners of vast ranch holdings, and lived in abandoned boats in San Francisco Bay. The so-called itinerant tramps and vagabonds who had crisscrossed the country's rail system in search of hard labor found themselves too late at every stop on their way west, from the Rockies to the Black Hills to Mexico, leading one carpenter to conclude, upon arriving in California: "Alas, the promised land is a myth."

DREAM AND I WALKED UP TO his dinghy, which was tied up at a harbor just north of Dunphy Park. It was a small wooden rowboat with a few life preservers shoved beneath the stern-side bench. "They're there if you need 'em," he told me as I climbed aboard. "But you won't."

I took a seat at the stern of the boat.

Dream climbed into the middle, and assumed a rower's position: knees together, legs pulled close to his chest, back hunched forward. He set the oars into their locks, and Bleau Bell jumped into the bow. As we pushed off from the dock, he told me he wanted to stop by his boat on the way to Bo's Fourth of July party. He needed to drop Bleau Bell off, he said; she did not like fire or loud noises and would need to nestle herself under his quilts and blankets to make it through the night. "I want to just feed you and you go to bed," he told Bleau Bell. "It's just *boom, boom, boom* tonight."

As we rowed out into the bay, I brought up the dead man Rose found in the park.

Dream frowned. "They think it's a murder and not a man who foiled himself to death."

I asked him what he meant.

"There is nothing there!" he shouted. He rowed faster and faster in silence.

I wondered why my question bothered him. Maybe he was worried that the man's death would be turned against them, more evidence that they didn't belong. Or maybe he just didn't care to dwell on the unavoidable risks to life on the water. There are some things you don't ask about, I recalled Larry saying.

We stopped first at Dream's boat. The hull was gray, no more than forty feet in length. Sheets of plywood covered the cabin's windows, and its walls appeared to have been erected haphazardly, like a birdhouse built for a woodshop class. As we reached the floating dock, Dream leaned toward me. "I'm gonna take a hit of LSD, just saying."

He climbed aboard, Bleau Bell following close behind, and the pair disappeared through the narrow cabin doorway.

I stayed out on the deck, listening to what sounded like cans rattling inside. Fastened to the transom was a small white trellis, through which a vine was growing up from a bucket of dirt. It was green and healthy, winding its way toward the sky.

Anchor-outs often had a plant in their charge. A plant or flower required little care, but it was easy to let these duties slip in low moments. It was reason enough to own one just to look upon it, when it was leafy and upright, and breathe a sigh of relief.

A few minutes later, when the noise settled down, I entered the cabin.

Dream was sitting on a bench affixed to the wall. Bleau Bell was curled up on a Persian rug on the floor. It was very dark inside, the only light coming through the rear doorway. Dream was staring at a milk crate full of paintings he had done. They were mostly seascapes and portraits. On either side of him was a mountain of brushes and squeeze-tube paints, as well as cans with dried-out drops of reds and blues and whites frozen along the sides.

He pushed open one of the wall panels behind him, and light filled the room.

He let it drop and it slammed shut; the room was dark again.

Across the cabin, he pulled a can of something from a shelf, opened it, and set it on the ground for Bleau Bell.

"I am a weirdo—the weirdo of my family," he said. He again lifted the panel that was covering the window and looked out across the anchorage, at the 250 or so beat-up vessels bobbing in the water.

The light was dimming. "The America that we live in is a commercialized America that is not really America," he said. "It's bizarre to even think about. The world that we live in has nothing to do with what we believe in. It's there to entertain us, for the benefit of policymakers. I can't put it into words, what I'm trying to say. The policymakers want it to be a slip-and-slide, something we slide on and don't recognize." Dream picked up a tall can of Heineken that was resting on a hot plate. "I'll drink this. That'll help." He sighed, reconsidering. "No, it won't." He reconsidered again, taking a sip of what must have been a very tepid, flat beer, and shook his head. "I'm lost."

A wave passed under the boat, perhaps from a passing craft, and the door swung open. "It was broad daylight, and I was getting drunk, drunk, drunk. I don't like to get drunk."

It's getting to that witching hour for fireworks, a voice on the radio said.

"I really don't give a shit about the fireworks," Dream said.

Every year, for what had become a very long time, he'd sit on his boat or another anchor-out's boat and watch the explosions in the sky, listening to the cheers of Hill People along the waterfront. Some were the voices of the kind old residents who brought him food in the park and always had a friendly word. Others were those of the police who dragged him to jail, or of the city council meeting commenters who demanded that his refuge on the water be destroyed. Each July, all of them came together to whoop and holler, shouting out across the bay. And none of it ever brought him any closer to shore.

At nightfall, we headed out for Bo's boat. We found him belowdecks, relaxing in the saloon with a young woman who, I gathered, was living there. She didn't give me her name but told me that she had cleaned up for the party: either side of the room had bright red pillows to sit on, and Christmas lights had been strung from the ceiling. The four of us climbed up onto the deck.

As the fireworks started, Dream shouted at the San Francisco skyline glowing across the water, declaring the spectacle a waste of money that could have been spent on the anchorage.

"Richard!" Bo shouted back. "Sit down!"

Bo handed me a can of warm beer, and I asked the young woman where she was from. She told me she had been visiting the United States from Russia, but she had overstayed her visa and was afraid to go back on land for fear the police would arrest her.

As the fireworks continued to explode, Dream continued to shout. Bo, getting drunker, continued begging him to stop. Once the show ended, I realized how late it had become. The bay was silent, and many of the lights on the hill had gone out.

I asked Dream for a ride back to shore.

We traveled in silence.

Watching him row, I thought he looked frustrated and tired, but also kind, and I also thought about how young he must have appeared when he moved onto the anchorage. I imagined him arriving from New Orleans decades earlier in search of peace of mind, a fresh start. But time had passed, and his teeth had rotted. The once-tolerant Hill People had turned against him. He now woke up each day in a creaky plywood boat, with empty pockets and a persistent cough, thoroughly on the second half of the chessboard. Happy or not, there was no going back to the old way of things.

Rarely did I hear anchor-outs talk about returning to the life they had before they came to Richardson Bay, or about finding a new life on land. Their concerns were always about the task at hand: fending off the RBRA, recovering from a storm, staying above water another day. Talking to them, I'd often wonder what they'd do if a chance to get off the water somehow presented itself. Never did it seem fair to ask.

When we arrived onshore, he gave me a big grin and tipped his hat.

I told him I hoped to see him again soon.

"It doesn't matter!" he said, offering me a friendly wave.

As he floated away into the dark and fog, I walked back to the bus stop, happy to know where I was headed.

6

THE FALL AND WINTER HAD PASSED WITHOUT CHANGE. IT WAS NOW 2016, a year after I'd first visited the estuary, and the Sausalito City Council, too, was in a holding pattern.

Though anchor-outs continued to clash with the RBRA and Sausalito, the overall size of the anchorage, about two hundred crafts, remained the same.

One evening in May, the members convened to once again revisit the now nine-year-old state law requiring the city to rezone a parcel of land for an emergency homeless shelter. The previous year, they'd ruled out the proposed sites, owing to their proximity to schools. Low on options, they were considering the greenspace and parking lot of City Hall itself. Each week the anchor-outs gathered for Pirate Church at this site adjacent to the concrete patio.

The chamber was packed with Sausalitans.

Before the discussion began, the council opened the floor to public comment.

Jeff approached the microphone with his Torah.

"We are now in the week of Acharei Mot," he said, adding that Acharei Mot meant "after the death of," a reference to the immolation of Aaron's two elder sons, Nadav and Avihu. They violated God's law by, in their zeal, lighting the fire for a sacrifice instead of ceding the task to Aaron. Their death was often interpreted as a story of the struggle between two forces of the soul: its *ratzo*, which is its desire to run away, to transcend material life; and its *shov*, which is its desire to settle down and achieve in the physical world. Nadav and

Avihu's *ratzo* overpowered their *shov*, and so, in a burst of flames, they departed the material world.

"I think this has some bearing on the anchorage," said Jeff.

He opened the Book of Leviticus.

"Aaron is the anointed one—he's Moses's brother. It says he, Aaron, shall take two he-goats, before the Lord at the entrance to the tent of meeting. And Aaron shall place lots upon the two he-goats. One lot says 'for the Lord' and the other lot says 'for Azazel.'"

Azazel is often interpreted as a fallen angel.

The he-goat for the Lord, Jeff explained, was to be sacrificed. "The he-goat upon which the lot for Azazel came up, will be placed, while still alive before the Lord, to initiate atonement upon it and send it away to Azazel, into the desert. Aaron shall lean both his hands forcefully upon the live he-goat's head, confess upon it all the willful transgressions of the children of Israel, all their rebellions, all their unintentional sins. He shall place them on the he-goat's head, he shall send it off into the desert. The he-goat thus carries upon itself all their sins to a precipitous land."

Jeff looked up to make his appeal to the chamber.

"All of us, I think, sometimes want to take what we see in the mirror and we want to point a finger at someone else. And sometimes that person, here in Sausalito, California, is a person who represents a lineage that was here long before the houses were. And that is the sailors, the mariners, now called the anchor-outs of Richardson Bay."

"Thank you," said the mayor.

Jeff wanted the council to understand that the anchor-outs were not squatters clogging the estuary, preventing its use by seafarers in need of shelter along their journey. No, they were those seafarers themselves, and the anchorage existed to protect them.

Eager to move on, the city clerk reviewed the state law meant to address the lack of shelter zoning in many of California's wealthy enclaves. "The staff found that the City Hall site and the corporation site were the most feasible to support two twenty-bed shelters in the planning period," she said. "Although the City Hall site could potentially support two shelters at one time—one in the parking lot and one in the park."

"Where did the number twenty come from?" asked a council member.

"The number twenty is the maximum number of beds in our existing adopted ordinance that a shelter can have," said the clerk.

"Could we change that—if we wanted—to twenty-five?"

"Yes."

"Okay, and so if we changed that from twenty to twenty-five, then the number of shelters that we would have to provide capacity for—not build, just show that it is possible to at some future point—could be reduced to one, couldn't it?"

"Correct."

Reducing the number of beds from forty to twenty-five failed to satisfy many residents at the meeting.

A man in a Giants jacket took the floor. "Among the chronically homeless, almost 30 percent of them are severely mentally ill. Almost 50 percent of them have substance abuse problems. These are people that can't get ahold of their lives. They're the people San Francisco shuttles over and drops them off at our doorstep. Because they don't want to deal with them. And so potentially, if you have a twenty-bed, or a twenty-five-bed facility at the city corporation yard, you're having five to six people who are mentally disturbed, half of them with drug abuse problems, who are going to be sitting there for ninety days or more watching kids walk by. . . . We've already had one murder on Nevada Street, by a man who was mentally ill. He killed his landlord. And then he killed himself in prison. And he lived there."

The man leaned into the microphone.

"Go Giants! Go Dubs! Go Sharks!"

The room cheered.

"Thank you," said the mayor.

Applause continued as residents echoed the man's concerns.

Later, a slight woman took the microphone. "Year after year, thousands of homeless people die due to exposure to the cold because certain people didn't care enough to go to the lumberyard and build an emergency shelter. It doesn't cost much to save a life. Anyone who needs shelter has the right to have shelter in a safe neighborhood. Any one of us could become homeless by way of a home being destroyed, loss of a job. A Sausalito shelter needs to be built. Most homeless aren't mentally ill or on drugs. And people have no right to treat them as such. Homeless people have the right to their freedom. They have the right to live outside of jails. And outside of barbaric mental institutions. Most homeless people have simply fallen on hard times. And they just need a hand up."

"I have *enormous* empathy, sympathy," said a council member.

Jeff grew angry at the response. He said to the council, "I know, and you know, that Sausalito has no intention of building a homeless shelter in 2016. I know and you know that there was not a chance of a homeless shelter being built, no matter what the audience said, no matter what you said. And yet we had to go through forty-five minutes of hate speech. I heard the homeless were responsible for murders—although it was somebody I guess killing his landlord, that means he had a place—sexual predators, thieves, mentally ill, etc. What this means is there is an attitude that needs adjustment. It's the easiest thing in the world to do. It doesn't take a dime."

Each week Jeff read from the Torah, hoping to show the city council members a path toward sharing the waterfront with the anchor-outs. But the tickets and arrests continued. Had they not listened to Leviticus? Did they not see that within them, the *shov* was overpowering the *ratzo*? Must the anchor-outs be the scapegoat for a sin not of their own making?

"I thought I did a good job of trying to convey about the goats," he said to the mayor. "*One of the goats is set free!* And he's not thrown over a cliff! Though he's in a land of precariousness, *he lives.*"

"Thank you," said the mayor.

Jeff put his hands out toward the council. "So I'm going to say—"

"Moving on," the mayor interrupted.

Bewildered, Jeff stepped back from the microphone.

If Sausalito was intent on scapegoating the unhoused, on making them suffer for property values, then he hoped the council heeded his reading: There were two ways to go, *two* types of scapegoats. One was sent to the tabernacle and killed. But the other was allowed to live, albeit at a distance, under the weight of the world.

7

BY THE END OF 2016, THE ANCHOR-OUTS WERE BUCKLING BENEATH THAT weight.

On a September afternoon, while Bo and I were listening to his radio in Dunphy Park, he told me that the mood on the estuary had changed. It wasn't just the RBRA, he said. Some new arrivals on the water were less interested in community than anonymity. With them came fights and break-ins, stolen dinghies, and unwanted attention. At his age, Bo was ready to get off the water.

"I started thinking differently," he told me. "I had this acid trip not long ago. The wind was blowing, and every time it blew things changed. I turned into a skeleton, and I thought, 'One hundred years from now this will be dust.' I was thinking, if only I could paint some of this."

He wanted to record his place and time before it vanished. So he began sleeping at a friend's house on the shore. To fund his paintings of the estuary, he sought out odd jobs on the hill. "I tell them, 'Excuse me, it's five thirty. I got to go home—like the white people.'"

Bo grew up in segregated North Carolina and had moved to Sausalito fifty years earlier, when many Black working-class boat-builders still lived in the area. Though I'd heard white anchor-outs claim that their community was "the most diverse group of people in the world," Bo was one of the few Black residents I'd met.

Later that afternoon, a well-dressed woman approached him and handed him a Steel Reserve. "Thanks, Bessie," he said.

Did he miss the water? I asked.

Bo cracked open his beer. On calm days it was heaven, but the world was intent on making it otherwise. "Everyone tells you how bad it is out there, how you don't have a bathroom. They don't let you enjoy it. Everyone is so hung up on toilets. You gotta show people there's another place in the world other than where they live."

He looked out on the bay.

"Things change fast," he said. Not long ago, Rose had left. "Her boat sank, and she had another baby. I think some other boat might have hit it—might have put a hole in it. They got it up a few times, but then they let it go. She wanted to go home anyway."

What finally made him leave?

"Larry and Ale," he told me. "Both those guys died."

A few months earlier, while Larry was smoking a joint, he started a small trash-can fire. When he leaned over to extinguish the flame, his beard ignited, which in turn ignited his oxygen tank, burning the inside of his throat.

I thought about the ninety-one-year-old not dying from natural causes. Ignore your doctors, he'd advised me. And it had worked for him. He'd survived for half a century on Richardson Bay, ingesting what he wanted, living however he pleased. He outlasted the average member of the top 1 percent by about four years, only to be felled by a roach.

I told Bo it sounded horrible.

"Larry tried to paint real life. People couldn't deal with it. They wanted flowers."

Then there was Ale, a seventy-eight-year-old Navy veteran who came to the bay in 1957. In recent years, he'd been anchored out in *Yesterday*, a World War II rescue boat where he stored his collection of discarded things found along the waterfront. After growing tired of a life of drinking, one day he began boiling the alcohol out of his Sierra Nevada stouts. He died of pneumonia in a VA hospital.

Toward the end, a resident of Gate 6 told a local obituary writer that he looked "like a gold miner from the 1800s."

"Now I might be the oldest—shit," said Bo. "My birthday's coming up. I'm getting ready to go." Soon enough, every anchor-out gets his or her funeral. "They make a boat for you. Everyone puts what they got to say to you on it. And they push it out and light it on fire. It's a pretty good send-off," he said. "It's like the Indians. They put the ashes on the boat. If you keep the ashes in an urn, you keep the man locked up. And he might come back someday. Shit, he might be back now."

Lately, I told him, there had been a lot of funerals.

"I've seen people go missing for two weeks. They float under the pylons. It's not people killing people, it's natural causes. You never know when it is going to end."

What did he mean by "natural causes"?

"I was talking to a girl one night, and the next day she hung herself. My best friend did the same thing a couple of weeks ago. I thought, 'No fucking way.' I didn't see any signs of him feeling bad."

THE AIR BLOWING IN OFF THE water was chilly for September, so I ducked inside the No Name Bar to warm up.

On the back patio, a few older men were gathered around a television. They were watching the first presidential debate between Hillary Clinton and Donald Trump.

The two candidates were fighting over whose economic plan would create more jobs:

> CLINTON: Let's stop for a second and remember where we were
> eight years ago. We had the worst financial crisis, the Great
> Recession, the worst since the 1930s. That was in large part
> because of tax policies that slashed taxes on the wealthy, failed

to invest in the middle class, took their eyes off of Wall Street, and created a perfect storm. In fact, Donald was one of the people who rooted for the housing crisis. He said, back in 2006, "Gee, I hope it does collapse, because then I can go in and buy some and make some money." Well, it did collapse.

TRUMP: That's called business, by the way.

CLINTON: Nine million people—nine million people lost their jobs. Five million people lost their homes. And $13 trillion in family wealth was wiped out. Now, we have come back from that abyss.

I looked around the patio. Almost everyone watching probably had an investment portfolio. And the Dow Jones Industrial Average and the S&P 500 had both increased over 50 percent since the eve of the financial crisis. In the same period, the number of unhoused people living on the anchorage, just across Bridgeway, had doubled.

A pink cockatoo caught my eye, strutting across the table next to me.

"Its name is Chinook," one of the men told me. "After Chinook salmon!"

As the debate went on, two men smoking cigarettes together began talking about the number of unhoused people living in San Francisco, which is estimated to be around ten thousand.

"If you go to sleep on the city sidewalk, everyone has to agree you are an indigent and you can't handle your housing," said a man in cabana wear and a panama hat. He suggested that the city move its unhoused population to Treasure Island, a landfill island built in San Francisco Bay for the 1939 World's Fair.

The other man smiled. "You will have your very own tent and a place to defecate."

AFTER I LEFT THE NO NAME, I took a walk down Bridgeway. I spotted Keven and Dream in the shade of an oak tree. I hadn't spoken to them in months.

Dream looked as I remembered, his skeletal frame animating a baggy T-shirt.

Keven, on the other hand, I might not have recognized. Little trace remained of his life as a sailor. His hair was down to his shoulders and his beard was long and wild. A crystal pendant swung from his neck as he paced back and forth in a pair of Jordan IVs, his knotty walking stick in hand.

I was sorry to hear of all the deaths recently, I said.

Keven nodded and pointed toward the burial ground. "We had a guy wash up two weeks ago," he told me. "It was a suspicious thing. The sheriff said he didn't know how to swim. But his family said he did."

What did they think killed him?

"Acute lumber poisoning," Keven said. "That's what happens out here. Someone just whacks someone in the head with an oar."

He really thought the guy was murdered?

Keven shrugged. "Things are coming to a head."

How so?

Dream leaned in: the Coast Guard had just executed a raid on the anchorage, he told me. Two anchor-outs were caught with meth, and many more were cited for safety and environmental violations. "They were practicing."

For what?

They told me to follow them out to the boat of a man named John.

THE SIDES OF DREAM'S WOODEN DORY were warped and had turned the color of a rotten banana. He was sitting toward the stern, hunched over. Bleau Bell was perched behind him.

I stepped in at the bow.

Dream warned me and Bleau Bell to stop moving, since the boat could capsize easily.

The pit bull ignored him, and we rocked violently on the trip out. When we arrived, and after Dream had secured us, she hopped off, ran across the deck to a pile of pillows and blankets, and fell asleep on top of them.

John's boat was just over one hundred feet, with a white steel hull and a single wooden mast whose sail had been removed. John was a small but durable man, wearing well the forty-six years he had lived out on the water. He met us on deck.

We followed him down to the galley, where a few anchor-outs were crowded over a hot plate, perusing shelves of canned goods. They were drinking jars of gin and cooking beans and rice. The only light came from a small wood-burning heater at the far end of the hull, around which a few anchor-outs were gathered.

Melissa and Innate were sitting on the couch. Across from them was a man in a tie-dye shirt and a young guy digging through cigarette packs piled on the coffee table, asking if anyone had seen his weed.

Innate stood up to give me a hug. He was wearing a bathrobe.

"It was a sorry thing," he said of Larry's death. "There has been a lot of turnover."

After Larry's passing, he and Melissa handed over their boat to Larry's wife, Diane, who took charge of the cats, along with three others she had brought along with her. The fate of Goofy and Broad was unknown.

The couple told me they moved onto a forty-five-foot shrimping vessel, which they liked just fine. Its steel hull was still filled with the foam that was once used to stabilize it on trawling trips and now made it uniquely seaworthy in stormy weather.

I told Innate he looked exhausted.

"I've gone through depression," he said. Recalling the moment Larry passed, Innate told me: "He anticipated the creator to amaze him. He was staring through the ceiling, and he would just start pointing."

I wondered what Larry saw through the ceiling.

"He was at this point when it was okay," Innate said. "He would often say, 'When it comes, sayonara, muchachos.'"

The room became quiet. Bleau Bell jumped up onto the couch and collapsed behind Innate and me. The guy in the tie-dye shirt sat up from his chair and shouted, "Distractions are mandatory!"

The young anchor-out asked again whether anyone had seen his weed.

"Sorry," everyone said, laughing as they passed around a bowl.

Keven descended the ladder carrying two large grocery bags.

John offered him a plate of rice.

He declined as he sat down next to me and began unpacking stacks of reports, printouts of emails, maps, and photographs onto the coffee table.

"We're not just walking around saying things are fucked up," Keven said to me, his fists full of papers. "Things are really fucked up." The pollution in the bay, he said, was worse than even they had realized.

John put two candles down on the table. I noticed for the first time a yellow flower in a vase of water. He walked over to a dresser drawer and began sifting through it. "This place is worse than an industrial site," he shouted over his shoulder. "Seventeen people have gone to the hospital since they started dredging."

Keven began talking about the hundreds of thousands of gallons of wastewater that regularly overflowed into the estuary during heavy rains, when the county's sewage system was overwhelmed. In 2008, for instance, a single storm washed in over two million gallons of raw sewage from the South Marin Sanitation District. Dozens of smaller spills occur every year. Between 2011 and 2013, almost three hundred thousand gallons reportedly had flowed into the bay from Marin residents.

John returned and dropped a two-volume draft of an environmental impact report for Waldo Point. Now, he said, they could prove it.

I looked the document over. It was covered in dirt, its pages separating from the binding. The date on the cover was 1997.

This is two decades old, I told him. It wouldn't say much about the conditions of the bay today.

Keven shook his head; he was sympathetic to my ignorance. "It took a couple of years for me to believe what Innate said. I didn't want to admit I wasted the first fifty years following a government that's corrupt. But it's true."

"But they're trying to blame us!" Dream shouted.

Keven laughed. "It's as if we could produce that if we all threw our shit into the water at once."

Hadn't the Hill People always complained that the anchor-outs were destroying the estuary? Why the sudden concern?

Because history, said Keven, was about to repeat itself.

How so?

Over the light of a candle burning on the coffee table, Keven and the others tried to explain. At a recent Sausalito City Hall meeting, they began, the RBRA's secretary called the anchorage a "clear and present danger" and requested a more than 50 percent budget increase to enable the harbormaster to "pivot towards an enforcement and abatement-based program." A council member then responded by declaring that an even heavier hand was needed: it was time "for the sheriff's office and the Sausalito Police Department to step in"; soon, the council member said, the police would begin enforcing a decades-old city law prohibiting boats from anchoring in its waters for more than ten hours. And to make matters worse, as of late, the Marin Audubon Society had joined with those calling for the eviction of the anchor-outs. The group's president had said that they lived in "violation of the public trust" and threatened the ecology of the estuary. Removing boats was no longer enough. Instead, she called for "strong enforcement" by the police.

Why does it matter, I asked, what the Audubon Society thinks?

Keven shook his head: I should try to pay better attention, he said. The Audubon *was* exactly what mattered. Didn't I know the story of the Houseboat Wars? Real estate interests might have motivated the clearing of Arques's waterfront, but it was carried out under the guise of environmentalism. The war, by some accounts, began when an inspector cited houseboats for code violations. But the codes didn't in fact apply to boats. Efforts by developers to sue houseboaters also failed, as did aggressive tactics used by county sheriffs. It was the BCDC, and its authority to enforce environmental laws, that ultimately provided the legal cover for evicting many of the waterfront residents, clearing the way for new million-dollar houseboats.

"It is a perversion!" Innate shouted, the light flickering on his face. The wealthy on land were the ones destroying the estuary. It was how they got wealthy to begin with. And yet the poor were the ones who would suffer for it. "There's a blister here, and when you pop it, you can really start following the festering."

John nodded. "We lost eleven people last year. A lot of people died because they were sick. As soon as they started dredging, people got sick."

I asked how many anchor-outs believed that the dredging had caused illnesses on the estuary.

"Out of about 120, perhaps twelve or fifteen," John said.

I looked around the room. There must have been eight or nine anchor-outs there.

"Most aren't really interested," John said. "They are in their own world."

After we finished eating, Innate and Melissa offered to give me a ride back to shore on their dinghy. The two of them looked cold and ready to get off the water, but as we approached the shore, Innate perked up. "Did you see that?" he asked me, pointing up at the sky. "A shooting star."

I hadn't.

8

LATER, I LOOKED UP WHAT INNATE HAD SAID THAT NIGHT, ABOUT THE RE-
gion's cities and wealth being built on the destruction of the bay.

In the 1850s, only the companies that could blast the earth
from the hills had access to gold. They used dynamite and gravity-
powered hydraulic hoses whose five-thousand-pound jets of water
easily shattered rock and uprooted forests, filling the rivers with mud
and toxic chemicals that washed out into the bay. Mine superinten-
dents, meanwhile, dumped eight hundred thousand cubic yards of
roasted cinnabar into creeks, poisoning the western Santa Clara Valley. And by 1855 hydraulic mining had so flooded the Yuba, Feather,
and American Rivers that mud and gravel were spilling out into
the Sacramento Valley before draining eventually into San Francisco
Bay. This flooding continued, and by 1862 the governor-elect had
to be rowed from his home to his inauguration.

Meanwhile, during San Francisco's financial crisis, city officials
paid off creditors by selling public land for cheap. Much of it was
underwater. State legislators carved up new lots on the bottom of
the bay and, just as they had done a few years earlier, allowed the
city of San Francisco to auction off the lots to the highest bidder in
exchange for 25 percent of the sale. The new owners dumped dirt
and rock into the bay, creating ever more valuable waterfront, at least
for a few years, until the whole process repeated itself once more. By
then, the legislature had also passed a bill allowing the sale of public
marsh, swamp, and tidelands to private interests, at the price of one
dollar an acre, paid in gold coin, to promote the curious environ-

mental cause of "agricultural reclamation." Limiting each buyer to 320 acres guaranteed that the resulting companies would be relatively small, and for a very brief time they were.

These companies seeded the tidelands with popular East Coast oysters, but in the northern sections of the bay, like Sausalito, the oyster beds failed to take hold. The value of the newly privatized lands nevertheless subsequently increased twenty-five-fold. And in places farther south where oyster beds were successful, the companies quickly consolidated, and the value of the landholdings grew a thousand-fold. When those oyster beds were finally so poisoned by the pulverized quartz runoff from hydraulic mining operations that they had to be shuttered, the beds were simply sold to cement manufacturers, which harvested their shell deposits. By the time the state legislature put a stop to the privatization of the bay in 1878, some fifty thousand acres of tideland had been transferred from the public trust.

In this way, cities and private developers continued to fill the waterway. In the century following the Gold Rush, an average of four square miles of the bay were lost each year to development. In the twentieth century, the slogan "Bay or River?" was adopted by the fledgling environmental movement as it lobbied the state to halt the shrinking of the coastline. When in the 1960s the movement finally succeeded and the Bay Conservation and Development Commission was formed, a full one-third of the acreage of the bay had been filled.

Though the BCDC was established in 1965, the idea of a consolidated governing body for the Bay dates back to at least the aftermath of the Great Earthquake and Fire of 1906. In the months that followed the disaster, the damage, in today's dollars, was estimated to be about $10 billion. Only 20 percent, however, was from the earthquake itself. As residents were quick to notice, the vast majority of the destruction resulted from the fires that followed. Causes varied, from home cooking with damaged chimneys to ruptured gas mains. The inferno was also exacerbated by homeowners who, after realizing their homes were insured for fire but not for earthquakes, began burning their houses. Hydrants, which were supplied by the city's privately owned Spring Valley Water Works, had offered little more than a trickle to extinguish them. The result was catastrophic. For days, air blowing in from across the water on three sides of the city produced updrafts that pushed the smoke a thousand feet into the air. By some accounts, three-story buildings vanished but for their cellars in as little as twenty minutes. With no help from Spring Valley's water system, soldiers rushed in with dynamite and tried to create a firebreak by blowing up homes surrounding the blazes, hoping to contain the inferno. But so hot and dry had the air become that a single burning ember from the blasts could bring down a city block in a matter of hours.

Spring Valley's failures were in part unavoidable. The quake had ruptured not only water mains but also the steam pipes needed for pumps to function. But once they were repaired, more systemic issues became apparent. The city was running out of water. The solution long ago proposed for this eventuality surfaced once again: dam the Hetch Hetchy Valley in the Sierras, allow the Tuolumne River to flood it, and direct the water via aqueduct 160 miles to the Bay Area. The problem remained that the privately held Spring Valley couldn't raise the capital. The fire, however, by reducing San Francisco's manufacturing output to 1899 levels, had increased the motivation of city officials to act. And the city's population had not rebounded as hoped, coming in at only 416,000 in the 1910 census. As a result, the movement to consolidate the cities of the Bay Area began to grow; operating as one municipality, the combined populations of San Francisco, Oakland, Berkeley, San Rafael, and San Mateo could raise the public funds to bring water to the region. City planners also argued that consolidation would put the metropolis on par with Chicago, which had recently annexed the entirety of Cook County, and with New York City, which a decade prior had consolidated into the five-borough system.

The plan to form a greater San Francisco was, according to its proponents, necessary and inevitable. The looming completion of the Panama Canal would open up the Bay Area to the arrival of waves of European immigrants; up until that point, most immigrants from Europe had arrived on the East Coast. With the opening of the canal, a ticket from Italy to San Francisco would cost only seven dollars more than the same trip to New York City. For merchants downtown, an influx of immigrants would exacerbate what they already deemed a crisis: the city center would become increasingly impoverished as the wealthy continued to flee to Marin's municipalities, like Sausalito, that were insulated from the working class by the high cost of rail and ferry transport across the Golden Gate. Consolidated regional planning was needed to handle the projected increases in demand for roads, trains, and water. California had by this point more than ninety thousand registered vehicles, and the ferry companies traversing the East Bay were already operating at capacity during rush hour. If the region was to grow, San Francisco insisted, it would have to grow as one.

San Francisco's arguments for consolidation were the same as those spoken against it in Berkeley, Oakland, Richmond, and San Rafael. The same census that showed only moderate growth for San Francisco showed a 120 percent increase for Oakland. Why, Oakland's leaders wondered, would they hitch their wagon to a stalled horse? And when officials in San Francisco argued that Oakland residents relied on them for employment, Oakland only had to run the numbers to see that this wasn't the case: according to one study at the time, only 6 percent of the East Bay population worked in San Francisco. Furthermore, Oakland's credit was pristine, while San Francisco politicians were so notoriously corrupt that they had somehow bankrupted the city during its own gold rush. Case in point: according to the claims of Oakland's leaders in the papers, they had discovered that Spring Valley was "promoting the plot" behind the scenes. The company's motive was to push forward the consolidation and the Hetch Hetchy Valley project, which would then require that the greater San Francisco area purchase the company for a projected $38 million. Why should the East Bay pay for the private utilities disaster that San Francisco had created? Only three counties would ultimately vote in favor of combining the region into a single city: San Mateo, Marin, and San Francisco.

San Francisco was left with no choice but to build the Hetch Hetchy dam on its own. Over the course of twenty-four years and seven bond measures totaling more than $140 million, the city dammed the valley, which had been inhabited for six thousand years by Indigenous tribes. They poured more than six hundred yards of concrete and seven hundred pounds of steel into the effort. The first water did not reach San Francisco until 1934. The delay was due, in part, to the First World War; for the duration of the war, civil engineers and workers turned their attention to the Sausalito waterfront, building Liberty ships for the war effort. But ultimately, East Bay officials would be proven right in their skepticism of the project. They would build their own hundred-mile aqueduct from the Mokelumne River—in one-fifth of the time, and for about one-fourth of the cost of the Hetch Hetchy dam. The total price tag of $39 million was just shy of what San Francisco paid in 1930 to acquire the Spring Valley Water Works alone. Los Angeles, meanwhile, was able to build an aqueduct nearly a hundred miles longer than the Hetch Hetchy line, for one-fifth the cost in one-fifth the time.

That so much public money could disappear into the hands of private contractors on such a vast scale might have been of more concern to San Francisco's leaders if not for the astounding profits the city generated from Hetch Hetchy. To this day, the city pays the federal government $30,000 each year for use of the valley while generating annual profits of $500 million from the sale of the water.

Oakland would not soon forget the lesson. As a result, efforts at regional planning among the counties of the Bay Area continued to falter for decades as the cities of the bay acted independently and in their own competing interests. Not only did the bay become more polluted, but unchecked filling, justified by a law meant to drain swamps in Louisiana, was reducing overall bay water quality by destroying the tidal flats and shallows that had the largest oxygenating capacity in the system. Meanwhile, both sides feared the completion of the Bay Bridge. Oakland was concerned that the bridge might steal retail trade, and San Francisco feared that shortening the commute to its business district would allow more taxpayers to move across the bay. And just about every fear harbored by the cities of the bay was realized. In the entire decade of the 1930s, San Francisco gained only 142 people. Meanwhile, Marin County, in resisting the creation of a rail line from San Francisco, limited the influx of working-class people.

Throughout the war years, pollution in the bay continued, not only from shipbuilding but also, in the decades after the war, from rampant public and private filling of shallows to create new, ever more expensive waterfront real estate. By the 1960s, researchers had confirmed that all but 187 of the San Francisco Bay's nearly 500 square miles of bay floor was shallow enough to be filled, if filling activities were left unchecked. In 1965, with all hope for any sort of consolidation effort among the Bay Area governments shattered by the building of the Hetch Hetchy dam, the California legislature created the Bay Conservation and Development Commission, thus gaining almost veto-proof power to prevent the filling of the bay shoreline. In only a few years, however, developers in the extraordinarily wealthy bayside towns began to pressure their local officials to co-opt the powers of the government to protect the interests of the very real estate developers it had been designed to thwart. First, the BCDC was mobilized in the Houseboat Wars to evict the residents of the waterfront and destroy their homes. Further BCDC mission creep ensued as the anchorage grew. By the 1980s, it had emboldened the RBRA to declare the anchored-out vessels to be bay fill, and their inhabitants to be polluters, and then to evict them from the water. That this was not the intended purpose of the BCDC is an understatement. When one of the act's two authors was asked, in 2007, if he or his legislative coauthor or anyone in Sacramento in 1965 had ever intended for the agency to be used to seize and destroy the homes of the anchor-outs, he simply replied: "No."

PART 2

THE DIFFERENCE BETWEEN EXPECTATION AND REALITY

2017–2018

9

IN JANUARY 2017, AFTER I RETURNED TO NEW YORK, INNATE PHONED WITH some unexpected news.

"Hey, brother," he said. "Things are really wild in the world." He explained that his mother, who passed away in 2013, had left her house in San Diego to her five children. He'd forgotten all about it when, a few weeks earlier, he received word that his sister had sold it, and that he was entitled to one-fifth of the proceeds from the sale, about $80,000.

He thought of the money as a blessing until he tried cashing the check: the bank he visited wouldn't accept it unless he had an active account. But when he tried to open one, they demanded a state-issued ID that he also didn't have. His attempt to obtain identification was thwarted by demands for proof of address, which he could see no way of getting, despite having been fined countless times for living in Richardson Bay over the previous decade.

Exasperated, he had taken the advice to sign the check over to Melissa, who cashed it for him. It was the first time he'd had any money in decades, and for the next few months they were uncertain about how to spend it. He and Melissa rented a hotel room and enjoyed a hot shower for the first time in weeks. At one point, he planned to hire a lawyer to push his self-authored lawsuit through to the Supreme Court ("the only true court," he said). But in December, after a clerk refused to accept his suit because he printed it on the wrong color of paper, he decided instead to use his newfound wealth to buy a secluded plot of land in Arizona so that he and the other anchor-outs could, as he put it, "maintain a course outside the harshness."

Wasn't that what the anchorage itself was supposed to be?

It was *supposed* to be that, he explained. But the estuary had proven too rough a place. Even the most nautically adept anchor-outs were inherently vulnerable to the hazards of stormy weather, hull delamination, dry rot, and the 1 percent. Each of these concerns required money for new parts, labor, tickets, fees, and fines. One way or another, lending a hand to a neighbor on the anchorage had meant helping them get money, or helping them not spend money. That was not the dream he had hoped his sunburns and backaches would realize. "The essence of love," he said, "was perverted into: 'How can we make money?'"

I told him I wasn't sure I followed.

"Doctors making house calls stopped pandemics," he said. "But going to the hospital generated more money." So now there are no house calls.

I countered: Did it matter? Hospitals still worked.

"It's about the love element," he said. Once money became the motive, he argued, a community couldn't care for itself. The past few weeks had taught him that. After he received his inheritance, he tried to help people with it. When he found out Bo needed a new anchor, he bought him one. Only later did he discover that Bo had attempted to return it for the cash to buy a van.

Innate didn't blame him for doing that.

Another anchor-out needed a chain, which Innate bought for him. The same thing happened. Innate didn't blame him either. Maybe the anchor-out had a fine to pay, or maybe they wanted a nice meal or a good night's sleep in a hotel. The point was, it had gotten all backward: money was supposed to get people what they needed to stay afloat, but now they were forced to trade what they needed for more money. Everyone was in too deep to stop themselves from sinking.

Why, I wondered, would a patch of Arizona desert be any different?

Years of floating on the anchorage, researching his civil rights case by the light of a solar-powered car battery, had shown him that a person's rights were attached to owning land. If his boat had been a house on a plot of land, for example, the harbormaster would never have been able to board it without a warrant. He would never have had to argue that he had a right to urinate and defecate. With land, he could grow enough vegetables to sustain himself. He could store dry goods, fix up and sell old machines, and fortify his home. "I need to get out," he said. "Look at Don Arques. He tried. He ended up a broken man. I don't want that story for me."

Innate's plan to build a desert paradise lasted until January, when he received a response to an ad that he and Melissa had posted on Craigslist. It read: "WE'RE LOOKING FOR SOMEONE TO COMPLETE OUR CIRCLE OF LOVE AND JOIN US IN AN OFF-THE-GRID LIFESTYLE TO FIND A MORE CENTERED VERSION OF THE SELF." A woman in Texas had written back expressing interest, explaining that she had inherited two hundred acres of land from her grandfather. Her husband was "killed in a war," she said. And she was looking for a fresh start. After exchanging messages online, Innate and Melissa decided to move to Texas and enter into a relationship with her: he would adopt her children, and their new family would get their water from a nearby river and farm the land.

Was he ready for such a big change? I asked one evening on the phone.

"Yeah," he said. "Everyone gets a brand-new lease, a brand-new chance." He hoped it would be a second chance at fatherhood.

What about Melissa?

"I love Melissa tremendously. My love for her will come out in deeper meanings and ways."

Right, but adding another woman—

"A balance of the tides and all that stuff."

Truth was, he told me, he didn't know exactly how it would all go. But he was ready to get back to the farming of his childhood, when he worked with his stepfather in the garden. "I got a lot of great exposures," he said just before we hung up. "Picking cherry tomatoes and getting bit by a gopher snake and catching it and getting it good and angry and putting it down a gopher hole to kill a gopher."

IN FEBRUARY, INNATE CALLED BACK AGAIN. "Texas fell out," he said. "She was too into the whole BDSM thing."

He and Melissa had again set their sights on Arizona, but decided not to open it up to the anchorage. "I was like, wait, I don't want to create this environment, with this temperament, and have to be the cop. I don't want any part of that."

They found a forty-acre plot of land outside of Snowflake, Arizona. Its soil was soft, and they deemed it good for farming. Juniper trees grew atop a mesa of petrified wood, where Innate had detected what he called "a spiritual presence." Walking around, he and Melissa imagined their new life. Along the side of a hill, they'd plant Hass avocado trees, which are not grown in Arizona, but which Innate was determined to grow anyway. They'd plant onions and garlic and Asian pears, as well as corn, squash, and cucumbers, all to be watered from a well they'd dig, which would tap into the Coconino basin. Innate looked forward to returning to the task of designing a water heater: he'd acquire a used Jacuzzi tub, fill it with rainwater, and cover it with PVC pipe, painted black. He was certain that it would work. But just in case, he'd buy an electric water heater too and attach it to a twenty-four-volt battery recharged by solar and wind generators. For shelter, they'd live in a four-hundred-square-foot shipping container ("a fucking mansion") and cap the ends with French doors. "I don't really want to put in any skylights," he said. "Too many years of leaks on the roof."

After Innate and Melissa left the property, they drove around the area. Snowflake has about five thousand people and is mostly white and Mormon. Not far from town is a community of thirty or so people who suffer from chemical and electrical sensitivity. They live in modest wooden homes with few, if any, electronic devices. To the north of Snowflake are the reservations of the Hopi and Navajo peoples; just south is the reservation of the White Mountain Apache. "It's really spiritually charged," said Innate, who believed that made Snowflake, along with an annual Burning Man festival, a good market in which he could sell white sage, a type of salvia.

On their way back to the hotel, Innate and Melissa stopped by a liquor store attached to a gas station. Melissa walked inside to purchase cigarettes while Innate waited in the car. It was evening, and a light snow had just fallen. The air was dry and crisp, and Innate was breathing easier than he had in years. He called out to a man pumping gas in a nearby parking lot. "Do you live around here?" Innate asked.

"Yeah."

"Is it always like this?"

"Yeah, this is what it's like."

"Fantastic."

Melissa returned to the car with the cigarettes. She told Innate the pack was five dollars cheaper than in Sausalito; that night they made an offer on the land.

After making the nineteen-hour drive back to Sausalito, Innate and Melissa returned to their boat, but left it after one night. Innate had spent fifteen years on the water and did not want to do it anymore. They packed their bed and other belongings, including a small library of books and a few drawers full of clothes, and turned back toward Snowflake. He soon abandoned his plan to live in a shipping container. He had soured on tight spaces, and the tools required to modify a shipping container had turned out to be more expensive than expected. So the couple bought a small barn with two lofts inside. It had eight windows and more space than Innate had known in almost twenty years. He built a solar panel outside. He bought an all-terrain vehicle he named Jughead, and a hardy strain of avocado trees to plant on the hillside of his mesa, protected from the wind. A local contractor dug him a four-hundred-foot well, from which he could pump one hundred gallons a minute. It cost him the last of his inheritance. "In some ways I'm back to the position I was on the boat," he told me one evening in March. "But now I have as much water as I need."

In the months that followed their move to Arizona, Innate planted his orchard of avocado and plum trees and a nearby alpaca farmer gave them a spinning wheel and manure for their garden. The two baked garlic bread in a solar oven they built by lining a foam-insulated cardboard box. Innate pitched burlap over the barn to protect it from the sun's ninety-degree heat, built swamp coolers by mounting computer fans he'd collected on top of buckets of cool water, and purchased a wind generator. He traveled to California and saw his son for the first time in more than a decade.

As summer approached, however, a feeling that Innate described as "the difference between expectation and reality" began to set in. Not unlike life on the anchorage, Arizona was rife with challenges. Chipmunks and rabbits came for his vegetables. He bought a .22-caliber rifle to fend them off but could never manage to overwhelm their assault. He found out only too late that farmers in the open tundra sprayed their crops with a watered-down molasses mixture to strengthen their flowers; strong winds blew away most of the flowers on his trees. What was left on his plum and avocado trees was taken by a late frost. The day before I spoke to him on the fifth of July, he'd accidentally shot a hole in his roof with his rifle, gashed his ankle on a stray nail, and burned off two of his fingerprints on a pot of boiling water. But he planned to turn his fortunes around. He and Melissa were replanting their garden using food-bearing plants they purchased from Walmart with her EBT card. "There are setbacks," he told me. "Fortunately, there are food banks."

10

INNATE AND MELISSA CONTINUED TO RECEIVE WORD FROM THE ANCHOR-outs about the worsening situation back in Sausalito.

New estimates put the anchorage boat population at 250 vessels, an increase of 20 percent in three years that reflected, city leaders argued, the RBRA's failed efforts to enforce its ordinance banning live-aboards. There was no mention of the 47 percent increase in chronically unhoused people in Marin County over the same time period. The *San Francisco Chronicle* ran an opinion piece co-written by the board president of the Marin Audubon Society calling once more for the eviction of the anchor-outs. Compassion should be shown, the authors said, but the offshore residents could no longer be allowed to let their anchors drag along the eelgrass, a habitat of the bay's native invertebrates. Nor could they be allowed to store trash on abandoned boats or dispose of human waste in the bay. The solution was not moorings, or trash collection, or bilge pumps, or public restrooms—it was eviction. Once again, the Sausalito City Council passed a law allowing the police to evict any anchor-out they caught inside Sausalito waters for more than seventy-two hours.

Meanwhile, the chief of the Sausalito Police Department had begun attending city council meetings and publicly making the same observation Keven had shared two years earlier: no matter how much money the city gave the RBRA, and no matter how many boats the agency removed from the estuary, the number of vessels in the anchorage never declined.

Why, the council wondered, did the RBRA lack the will or the capacity to remove the anchor-outs?

When the RBRA first established its seventy-two-hour ordinance in the 1980s, there was little incentive to enforce it aggressively. The population on the water, including the western portion in Sausalito's jurisdiction, had remained relatively stable for years, at between ninety and one hundred boats. Many, if not most, were occupied by the people who set themselves the task of learning to handle the perpetual maintenance and repair that their watercraft required. In 2009, however, in the months after the financial crash, the anchor-out population began to swell, eventually accounting for almost one-quarter of the more than one thousand unhoused people in Marin County. Why this happened was a matter of debate, as no comprehensive surveys existed for the anchorage. However, surveys of the countywide population suggested that almost half of the anchor-outs were on the water as a result of job loss or eviction, and others came after divorces and breakups or to flee domestic violence.

Though the county's homelessness was often framed as transient and criminal, fewer than one-third of unhoused people could be so described. In fact, about 15 percent were employed but simply could not afford to rent a home, which required a salary of about $100,000 to do sustainably. Nevertheless, in the years following the Great Recession, as Sausalito's wealth grew, its political winds shifted and public opinion turned against the estuary's ballooning population.

"In January was the new marine debris law," the police chief said at the city council meeting months earlier when he announced the department's new anchor-out plan, as if he were spotting the first blossoms after a long winter. "It's actually a really great law that's on the books."

He went on to explain, using a PowerPoint presentation: according to a new state environmental law, the department would be vested with the authority to declare a boat marine debris and then it could classify the boat as waste instead of as a vessel. Once determined by a city employee to be garbage, an unregistered boat could be hauled away after a ten-day notice. Unregistered vessels could be dragged to the Army Corps of Engineers yard and crushed immediately. "We're looking forward to enforcing it," he said.

The chief as much as acknowledged the vagueness of the "debris" terminology used to connote protection of the environment. "We will probably be in a bit of a test case," he said. He noted that this approach would spark many disagreements with the anchor-outs on the question of whether their homes were in fact debris. But he reminded the council that the law "allows quite a bit of latitude." He offered a reassuring anecdote about an anchor-out they had recently arrested. When the man was in jail, "he didn't make any arrangements" for his boat. So the city was able to take it over and crush it before he was released. "We warned him."

The dire implications of the new law were clear to the anchor-outs attending the meeting.

One, Doug, took the microphone.

Although he was not currently living on the water, he had been for many years. In that time, he had tried to broker peace between Sausalito and the anchorage, to no avail. It was clear to him now, he said, that the city wasn't negotiating in good faith.

"I came out here to go to seminary," he said. "I fell in love with this area. I was called to this community. My roommate went to China. I went to Richardson Bay. I don't know which had the more exciting time in challenges of languages and culture." He laughed. "I don't have the time to go into the myriad countless presentations given. They are slanted, they are biased."

Doug was the record holder for the most dives in Richardson Bay. He'd seen firsthand the anchor-outs' environmental impact on the bay floor and conceded that the dragging of anchors on the eelgrass and the dumping of human waste in the water wasn't good for the ecosystem. But these impacts didn't compare to the damage done by the Marin County sewage flowing into the bay during rainstorms. To claim that the anchor-outs were the ones destroying the bay was, to Doug, absurd.

11

SINCE THE BAY AREA'S EARLIEST DAYS, THE WEALTHY'S RECOVERY FROM
financial calamity had come at the cost of the poor, transforming
the region in the process. It is in this history that the anchor-outs
find their origins.

In the mid-1850s, after the city's financial collapse, the somewhat
less rich bankers in San Francisco righted their affairs. They opened
new firms, often in the still-furnished offices of their failed Gold
Rush endeavors. A former cabinetmaker named William Ralston,
who made a modest fortune aiding in the overthrow of Nicaragua
and transporting ill-fated gold seekers to the tapped-out mines of
California, threw his lot in with three other businessmen to form
Garrison, Morgan, Fretz & Ralston in 1856. They put the bank's
money to work building grand hotels, running mills, and growing
factories for everything from furniture to fine watches. Ralston put
their chips on the one sure bet he'd spent the last decade nurturing:
the growth of San Francisco, which, when his bank opened, was
increasing in population by a quarter year over year. More people
meant more homes, more farms, more factories. New arrivals, no
matter how broke or disappointed, would need somewhere to live.
Ralston's firm became the most powerful in the city. His partners
came and went, retiring or running for office, as he all the while
bought shares in any enterprise he could find, leading one of his
colleagues to observe: "He knew practically every man in San Francisco." Things might have gone on like this as Ralston, a man loved
in his time and forgotten later, slowly and quietly built his Califor-

nia empire. But then, in 1859, a lode of silver ore was discovered in the Virginia Range of what was then the Utah Territory.

Mining of the Comstock Lode began like the Gold Rush a decade before. Miners made, bought, and traded claims, and in short order they had exhausted the ore along the surface that they could haul away with a shovel and a bucket. The belief in Virginia City was that the silver deposits had been depleted, as they had been in recent strikes along the range. California bankers, each with his own ears in the mines, believed this as well. Ralston, however, wagered otherwise. He bought up claims where he could. As silver mills refined less and less ore, their value dropped, and he bought them too. At a time when the going interest rate was as much as 5 percent, he offered 2 percent loans to owners of failing mines who wouldn't outright sell. They flocked to his bank, and when they failed, as he knew they would, he took possession. By 1864, when he founded the Bank of California, Ralston was already holding a near-monopoly on the Comstock Lode. Through the bank and his vast holdings, he attracted East Coast investors to his mining ventures. And once again the industrialists moved in: first to tunnel into the earth, then to timber-reinforce those tunnels when they proved to be prone to collapse on the miners. The deeper they dug, the more capital the operations required. Steam and hydraulic pumps were developed to draw out water hot enough to boil an egg. Compressed air drills with diamond heads were brought in. Underground transport networks conveyed wire-cable drawn cages. Lumber and sawmills were built on nearby mountainsides to grind out eighty million feet of timber a year to service not only the mines but the company camps that cropped up around them. A network of iron pipes brought in more than a million gallons of water a day from the Sierra Range.

As money and workers flowed into San Francisco from the Comstock Lode, the city sprawled out across the arid sand dunes. When freshwater creeks and springs dried up, private land speculators looked south and across the bay for irrigation. The groundwork

had been laid by then: the California legislature had created, in no-
torious secrecy, a pathway for a new and privately held water company to seize land through eminent domain, provided the land was
used to bring water to the thirsting metropolis. And seize it did: the
shareholders of what became the Spring Valley Water Works took as
much land as possible surrounding the city. Through the company,
they brought water to their holdings by damming and redirecting
the rivers and streams of San Mateo County. When one or another
new operation threatened their monopoly on the city's water and
land supply, they crushed and consumed it. Spring Valley provided
enough fresh water to turn the city into a major metropolis in only
a decade's time.

But the limits of that growth soon became apparent. By the
1860s, San Francisco was the only city in the world besides London
to control a water supply for more than fifty thousand people that
was held in private ownership. It was then that the idea of building
the aforementioned aqueduct from Hetch Hetchy had first taken
hold. But expanding the vast aqueduct system with new dams, canals, and tunnels into the Sierras was beyond the reach of private
capital. And so, in 1875, the San Francisco Board of Supervisors
voted to acquire Spring Valley Water Works, along with water rights
to Alameda Creek, which it planned to incorporate into the new
public system.

Before the sale could be made, word of the plan reached Ralston
in his office at the Bank of California. Ralston had by this time
built himself a reputation as a genial but shrewd and paradoxical
man who, as one colleague noted, "had a memory that ran to details
and yet in all his business dealings he seemed to shun them." It was
a disposition that at last was catching up to him. As his Comstock
fortune had grown, he'd put it to work back home, using the Bank
of California to make speculative plays on regional rails, canals, and
land in anticipation of the arrival in 1869 of the transcontinental
railroad. But when the trains did come, they failed to deliver on the

economic promise he had hoped for. As Ralston's bets got bigger and more speculative, he became overextended, saddling the bank with junk bonds and crushing debt. The Spring Valley deal, he surmised, offered a way out, albeit one of astounding illegality: Ralston preempted the municipalization of the water supply by first personally buying up the Alameda watershed rights and the Spring Valley Water Works. Because the Bank of California was the financial center of the West, no one questioned Ralston's issuance of stocks for the water company at an outrageous valuation. He then used the money raised from those overvalued shares to have Spring Valley purchase from him the Alameda watershed rights, netting himself a quarter-billion in today's dollars. The last step of Ralston's plan was to offload the bank's inflated holdings in the Spring Valley Water Works onto the San Francisco public. He structured a deal that would net enough to pay off the bank's debts and put an additional $137 million (in today's dollars) in his pocket.

However, San Francisco proved less willing to overlook the details of this arrangement than Ralston had hoped. In the course of its due diligence, a survey by the city revealed the scheme. The public was outraged, and the municipalization of the water company was halted indefinitely. Trust in Ralston evaporated, prompting a run that cleaned out the Bank of California. Ralston transferred his holdings to his business partner, William Sharon, and then left his office for his daily afternoon swim. That evening, his body washed up on the Larkin Street Pier. "Best thing he could have done," Sharon said at the viewing of his friend's corpse. The funeral, attended by thousands, was held a few blocks from the site of Ralston's $5 million luxury Palace Hotel, which upon its opening a few months later would be the largest in the world.

Ralston's failed scheme to sell the Spring Valley Water Works only cemented its monopoly. Public support for purchasing the firm had evaporated, leaving the city's leaders little choice but to abide by the whims of the company's directors. Unbound by municipal borders or customer satisfaction, Spring Valley increased rates so much that many San Franciscans simply stopped paying them. The company demanded the legal authority of a tax agency that was empowered to recover money to pay for public services. Accusations that it failed to provide those services were met with counter-accusations that the "populace" was "arrayed against wealth." All the while, factory workers and low-wage gold and silver miners overpaid for drops of water from the same watershed that flowed freely to the palatial estates of San Mateo County—water that was siphoned away from increasingly destitute farmers in Alameda County.

Those withering farms were among the first sights seen by the thousands of wounded, unhoused, and itinerant veterans of the Civil War from back east who were yearly arriving at the transcontinental railroad's Alameda terminus. Little is known about them, other than that those from the South were mostly white: tramping relied on kind white helping hands along railroads and their adjacent farmlands. Furthermore, southern landowners, aware that wages were about 15 percent higher outside the South, marshaled local political power to restrict the free movement of Black Americans by saddling them with insurmountable debt or passing so-called anti-vagrancy laws that allowed for the forced employment, for up to three months, of anyone police deemed itinerant. Those who tried to escape this employment were chained up and made to work for no pay. Companies throughout the region exploited the law by conspiring to pay Black workers less than they had paid enslavers before the Civil War. As regional wage drops spread nationwide, homelessness and poverty increased in turn. Cities across the country responded by adopting their own anti-vagrancy laws. More than a million people a year were being arrested for vagrancy by the mid-1870s. In municipalities across the United States, men and women on the streets were asked to give accounts of their travels; if their accounts were deemed insufficient, they were arrested, flogged, branded, or had their ears cut off. Newspapers in Chicago suggested that strychnine and arsenic be used to poison food given to the poor, the *New York Herald* suggested poisoning their food with lead, and the *Indianapolis News* demanded that they be stripped of the right to vote.

In the Bay Area, the full impact of Spring Valley's greed on the region's most vulnerable and destitute people wouldn't be realized until decades later, on the morning of April 18, 1906, as the earth beneath San Francisco began to shake. The shantytown shacks crumbled first, sending thousands into the night carrying bundles of bedding as children pulled wagons full of family photos and jewelry. Steamer trunks were abandoned when the hilly climbs through the city became too much. Many poor people buried their most valuable belongings in soft earth. The wealthy, meanwhile, forced their staffs, at bayonet point, to tow their wardrobes and furniture through the streets. Parks filled with unhoused residents; twenty thousand people camped in the Presidio alone.

When fires broke out, the city's dwindling water supply did little to extinguish the inferno. The staffs of the *Call* and the *Chronicle*, meeting at the offices of the *Evening Standard* after their own buildings burned down, wrote report after report on the nightmarish scene as it stretched on for days: horses screeching and panicking in their stalls; children running through the streets carrying their dogs dying from smoke inhalation; teams of rescue workers frantically searching for the dead as people screamed in protest, "What's the use?"; a woman running through a panicked crowd holding a parrot that could only say the word "hurry"; another parrot carried by another woman repeatedly saying, "This is the limit"; the baby of an Italian vegetable peddler crying next to a German man playing the fiddle; on the top of a hill, a bearded Italian man waving a chromolithograph of Francis and calling on the patron saint to save his city; crowds using umbrellas to scare charging horses; an old woman in Chinatown carrying a large box of love letters she refused to discard; a monk leaning over an Orthodox Jewish man and whispering words of comfort; wooden crosses being erected in the rubble for the dead; a Salvation Army lieutenant reporting on having heard that Los Angeles was destroyed, that Portland and Seattle were wiped out by a tidal wave, and that Chicago was completely underwater; Ralston's Palace Hotel, the crowning achievement of the banker remembered as "the man who built the city," crumbling to the ground; and a street preacher on Stockton Street stepping up onto his box and shouting: "Haven't I prophesied all of this? Haven't I told you this wicked town would be consumed?"

By the time the last embers of the San Francisco fire had cooled, more than twenty-eight thousand buildings were destroyed across nearly five hundred city blocks. More than half of the city of four hundred thousand had become homeless. The US Army rented circus tents to house tens of thousands in the Presidio. Meanwhile, it took only six days for a committee of city leaders to begin plotting to relocate the Chinese residents to Hunters Point, putting them as far away from the city as possible while still obligating them to pay taxes. Some of the newly unhoused made the journey across the Golden Gate to Richardson Bay, where they moved onto the abandoned fishing vessels and arc-boats that the Arques family kept on the Sausalito and Tiburon shorelines. These were the first anchor-outs to establish residence on the anchorage of Richardson Bay.

12

INNATE AND MELISSA PASSED THE LONG, HOT SUMMER OF 2017 IN THE desert, putting in a tree grove. They would ride Jughead into town, pluck saplings from the grassy islands of strip mall parking lots, and bring them home to plant on a well-irrigated patch of soil. We spoke less and less. Time for the phone was limited to the noonday hours, when they took off their clothes and gathered by the swamp cooler to wait out the sun. They imagined their life together, years in the future:

"It's gonna be super nice," Innate told me one afternoon in September. Soon they would gather up the dead juniper and cedar trees to burn on the cold winter nights to come. On the cleared soil, they would plant corn, "sweet and delicious—we're eating it right off the stock." They'd sketched out plans for patches of watermelons that Innate believed would grow to sixty pounds. He had another plot marked out for sugarcane, and another still for broccoli. "People say, 'I've never seen that growing around here,'" he told me. But that didn't mean it couldn't.

What if some plants wouldn't grow in the desert? I asked.

He allowed for that possibility. After all, his cilantro had died, and the carrots were in trouble. But his lettuce did fine, and his zucchini had grown up to his knees. To him, his patch of desert was like the legumes he planned on growing. "When it looks like the plant is dying, you break it open and there's a pinto bean inside!"

As the months passed, he'd stopped talking about terms of art in admiralty law and the New Deal efforts to expand the court system. He was no longer interested in the abuse of the BCDC's mandate and the powers that the US Coast Guard could or could not transfer to the harbormaster. "To hell with other people, with shitting into a doggy bag and carrying it to shore," he said.

His war had ended.

THAT FALL I RETURNED TO THE Sausalito waterfront.

Years had passed since Innate first showed me the wreckage of the *Galilee*. Many of the people I'd met that day were gone. The ship's remains, however, still looked about the same: old and tired, but like what was left might just hang on until it all vanished at once in the tide pool.

The *Galilee*, it is said, still holds the record for the fastest voyage from San Francisco to Tahiti: nineteen days. It arrived in Richardson Bay in 1936, when its owner sailed it up through San Francisco Bay and dropped anchor along the Sausalito shoreline. It never moved again. For many years, a retired sea captain and his wife lived there, followed in the fifties by another family. After they left, a few years later, the tides gradually wore away the boat's wooden hull, burying it beneath layers of rocks and sand. Today what remains of its skeleton is encased in a mound of grass. Crows perch on a portion of its mast jutting out from the earth.

When Larry first moved to the anchorage, the *Galilee*'s portholes would have only just stopped glowing. With him gone, no one was left to see in the schooner's wreckage anything more than a crow's nest with a good story. Looking at it, I thought back to the last afternoon I had spent with Larry and Diane on the *Evil Eye*. It must have been a year earlier . . .

"BACK THEN, THERE WAS A CABIN there, and part of the bow," Larry said, pointing through the wall. "Diane and I lived right next to the *Galilee*. In a place called Bob's Boatyard. In 1980, they built Galilee Harbor. The first step was they tore down Bob's."

Diane, seated beside Larry, perked up when she realized the topic. "They came in with workers on furlough from San Quentin," she said. "Early in the morning."

As we drank coffee with Handsome Harry, the pair recounted the city's first evictions of the waterfront residents. Early efforts relied on code violations, which the structures were certainly guilty of. Newspapers sided with the town in wanting to evict boatyard dwellers. They published stories noting the infractions and announcing that once construction permits were granted, demolition could begin immediately, without any notification. And that's exactly what happened. Years after the fact, onetime residents of Bob's Boatyard recounted waking up to the rumble of bulldozers and being given no time to gather their belongings before fleeing their homes.

"It was all totally illegal," said Larry. "Once they got away with that, they started moving north. They got rid of Gate 3," he said. "We put up a pretty good fight. I enjoyed it."

Diane nodded as they looked at each other.

Larry smiled and shook his long pointer fingernail at me. "There is something exhilarating about fighting against an unbeatable enemy."

Handsome Harry curled up at Larry's feet.

"There were parties everywhere in the neighborhood," he continued. "But the main party was on a boat called the *Van Damme* at Gate 6," he said. "They just came in one day and tore this beautiful old ferryboat down. That kind of took the heart out of the community."

I asked Larry if, after the waterfront was destroyed, he had ever thought about moving on, going somewhere else.

"I've been a lot of places. Where would I go? For a while, I wanted to go to Argentina to do the tango." He mimicked holding a partner with his hands, then sighed and fell quiet.

What was wrong?

"I'm trying to think. Is there still a place? I don't think so. A lot of places I would have wanted to go fifty years ago, but not now."

Like where?

"Cuba," he said. "It's opening up now. But in a way that means it becomes just another place. It'll change for the good in some ways, change for the bad in some ways. Like everything else."

What about New York? Had he ever thought about returning? He grew up there, in Brooklyn, in the back of his father's tailor shop.

"You can't go home again to New York," he told me. He said he'd led a whole other life there. Even gotten married.

I must have looked surprised. He spoke more, then got lost in thought before saying:

"Too many ghosts. Certain places, like Greenwich Village, no matter how it changed, it still has its own magic. I don't know what it is all about." Every once in a while, he said, for no reason, it just happened to certain places. "Jesus, Muhammad, Solomon. All these fucking crazies came out of the same place. I never did figure out why."

To Larry, Richardson Bay was like that.

"I met Watts about 1970. He died in '73. He used to help me get my car started every morning."

Alan Watts was an English-born philosopher who popularized Eastern religions during the hippie movement. He believed that humans were cruel to one another as a consequence of their isolation from the natural world. "Poor guy. He loved to drink. He loved to have a good time. He said he could get two books out of one acid trip. But after a while you get tired. I like Einstein and his whole shot, but if you get into the philosophical side, there is no end of the line. Serious things are too serious to be taken seriously. Serious for me is life and death."

I asked him what he meant by "serious."

His bare feet were propped up on the table. "I remember an acid trip I had," he said, stroking his yellow-white beard. "I was a sperm swimming through my mother's vagina—well, soon to be my mother—and I wasn't trying very hard at it. I looked around, and the other sperm were just floating around on their backs. And you can beat all the other sperm, but you can get there at the wrong time of the month, or end up down someone's throat or in their hand. To arrive at the right time—it's just so off the fucking wall. I don't have a religious thing, but there is something that got me here: the stuff that gets you here, against all odds. You're just floating along. You get there first, and they close the door."

I TURNED TOWARD THE SHORE. DREAM was walking in from the dock, not far from where Rose had found the dead man's body.

He must have tied up his skiff in Galilee Harbor. Twilight was settling in, and I was surprised to see him coming to land at this hour. He waved his hand at me.

I asked how he was doing. It had been a while since we'd seen each other.

Dream shook his head. Bo died, he told me. It was a heart attack. It had happened a few months earlier, in the summer.

Dream described the show of Bo's artwork that Sausalito residents had put on in his memory.

I said it sounded nice.

"They could have given it to him while he was alive," Dream said.

In the months after his death, residents shared the glimpses of

Bo's life that he had shown them over the decades. He was color-blind in one eye. He came to Sausalito in 1969 with the US Jobs Corp. He learned to paint in 2004, starting off with stick figures. A video of an interview Bo had given a filmmaker a few years earlier began to circulate. "I'm one of the greatest painters that can do color. And I'm color-blind in one eye," he told the filmmaker. "I'd see a lot of Picasso, a lot of that guy's stuff. Thing is, it's a drab, gray color. You don't want to look at that all day. That's how your mind goes."

In the months before he died, one resident said, he began calling himself Bocasso.

I asked Dream who ended up living on Bo's boat.

"Army Corps of Engineers crushed that thing up," he told me. When the town wanted to rid the bay of a vessel, it sometimes contracted with a wrecking yard to crush it. Other times, it turned to the Army Corps of Engineers, headquartered just up the coastline from Dunphy Park. The Corps had a yard on the water where they hauled boats onto land, attached them to a crane, and dropped them repeatedly until they were reduced to a pile of old wood, fiberglass, and the family photos, clothes, and other possessions that most anchor-outs had carried with them through life.

Dream looked up at the hill. "You really know who your friends are," he said. Bo had always warned him about that, he told me. "In fourteen years, I've lost twenty friends," he said. "Of all the things in this bay, I wish one thing was gone. The pirates." He was referring to the RBRA and the Sausalito police. "It's an operation. They want us to go ahead and have war so we can be violent and they can take us out."

Dream walked over to the wreckage of the *Galilee* and pointed to a spot by the fence. It was there, he said, that Bo told him he was having stomach problems. "I gave him his last drink of water."

At the time, he hadn't known it would be the last time he saw Bo.

"The day Bo died I was on my boat. I said a prayer that I wanted

Adam to change his ways," he said, referring to another anchor-out. "And then I prayed that Bo be at peace. And it was in that same time that Adam fell off his bike and Bo died."

Dream paused as if to let a thought run through his head. "And Adam is still a jerk, and Bo is dead. He was cremated and sent back to his home—in an urn—to North Carolina."

The anchor-outs, Dream said, sent Bo off as they did anyone who somehow ended up among them. They built him a boat, set it on fire, and pushed it out to sea.

13

IN 2017, MARIN COUNTY FOUND THAT WHILE THE OVERALL NUMBER OF
unhoused people had decreased from 1,309 to 1,117, the number of
those who were chronically homeless had increased from 281 to 329.
The chronically homeless, as many anchor-outs are, have spent more
than a year on the streets. They are often the most vulnerable, and
their circumstances may shorten their life spans by up to a quarter
of a century. Months earlier, the county had empaneled a civil grand
jury and tasked it with investigating the main cause of the increase
in chronic homelessness. Just before summer, the grand jury published its findings. The main cause, its members surmised, was a
lack of affordable housing. In Marin, they found, the median rent
for a one-bedroom apartment would require an income of $98,000,
based on the 30 percent income rule. The many whose incomes were
not that high were in danger of chronic homelessness.

The jury issued recommendations for each of the county's municipalities, to which their city governments were legally required to
respond. To Sausalito, where there are no homeless shelters, the jury
issued a simple recommendation: "Actively seek developers to create
housing for the homeless within their jurisdiction."

The city was required to respond to the grand jury findings,
though it wasn't in fact required to act on their recommendations.
The city council members drafted a response rejecting the jury's advice. They noted in the letter that, while they lacked the financial
means to create new housing, they had nevertheless been tackling
the issue. Once a year they held a health fair in the park, distributing

blankets, life preservers, clothing, and fire extinguishers. A police team, they wrote, had been "tasked with breaking down the communication barriers and creating an environment where someone in need would feel comfortable coming to the Sausalito Police Department for help."

FOR ITS MEETING IN MID-JULY, THE Sausalito City Council placed the adoption of the response on its consent calendar, which is reserved for items considered so agreeable and noncontroversial that they can be approved in one sweeping ruling, without debate or discussion.

"Any other public comment on our consent calendar?" the mayor asked.

An angry Jeff slowly approached the podium. He stood in silence next to a lone floor fan circulating the summer California heat in the mostly empty room.

"The reason that this beautiful system of designating leaders broke down was because the people and their—"

"Jeff," the mayor interrupted. Lately, Jeff had been talking a lot about the election of Donald Trump, and how it represented a city, state, and national crisis in which the poor and disenfranchised were robbed of their voices. The mayor feared he was at it again: "This is for comment on the consent calendar—"

"The item is 4B!" Jeff snapped back, referring to the plan to swiftly push through a response letter informing the Marin County grand jury that Sausalito would not seek to build a homeless shelter because it lacked the funds. "I see you have removed two items from the consent calendar, and I hope this is another one. Twenty million dollars! Ten million from the county and the cities and $10 million in matching funds from the feds is now being given, and has been for the last two years, to hire case managers for the 1,172 counted houseless people in Sausalito. That works out to almost $20,000 per person. The grand jury, which is composed of citizens that are not salaried, they are doing this because they care about their county, have come up with a number of solutions to houselessness. Good ones. Sausalito now wants to say they are not willing to sign on? All the services, except for very very few exceptions, in Sausalito, are accessed in Marin City, with much less population, but a big sense of solidarity."

Jeff's reference to Marin City was a pointed one.

The city's history dates back to Japan's bombing of Pearl Harbor in 1941, when the United States mobilized for war. Thousands of young men, including Larry, were signed up and sent to Hawaii to peel bodies from the wreckage. Meanwhile, the governor of California put out a call for a West Coast ship manufacturing yard to produce sixty ships for the war effort. The engineering and construction firm Bechtel Company bid on the entire project, proposing a yard in Sausalito. Despite having no shipbuilding experience, Bechtel received a contract from the government in less than two weeks. Forty homes that made up the Pine Point waterfront neighborhood were demolished and dumped into the bay to make way for the new project. Lands belonging to the Northwestern Pacific Railroad and the South Pacific Coast Railroad were bought as well. On top of that, twenty-six thousand pilings were driven into the bay. A shipping channel was dredged through the federal anchorage, displacing three million cubic yards of soil from the bay bottom. Onshore, a military freight line was put in to supply the efforts. Twenty thousand workers were brought into Sausalito just to construct the Marinship Yard, which included a 122,000-square-foot warehouse. Meanwhile, the smaller established local builders joined in as well. The Arques family retooled their yard to produce barges that were put to work hauling military equipment through the San Francisco Bay waterway. The Oakland Shipbuilding Company established a yard in Sausalito to fulfill military contracts. Even Sausalito's mayor, Herb Madden, who spent two years in prison for repairing rum-running vessels during

Prohibition, was given a Navy contract to manufacture torpedo boats. Steel was scavenged from old bridges and structures to feed the war machine. The first ship out of the Marinship Yard was christened the *William A. Richardson*. All told, some seventy-five thousand workers were brought to Sausalito for the effort.

Workers came from across the country to fill the new shipbuilding jobs. Arriving primarily from Louisiana, Arkansas, and Mississippi, Black workers tripled the Black population of the Bay Area during this time. Many moved to San Francisco's Western Addition neighborhood, which had been home to Japanese Americans until they were rounded up and imprisoned by the US government at the onset of the war. Black residents also moved to Hunters Point, home to the slaughterhouses banned in the city proper in the late nineteenth century; this was also the neighborhood where city planners conspired unsuccessfully to concentrate Chinese residents after the great fire destroyed Chinatown. In Marin, government housing was established, including in the newly formed Marin City, just north of Sausalito, where many Black workers were concentrated.

Billions of federal dollars flowed into the Bay Area during the war. Although federal defense contracts officially prohibited racial discrimination by recipients, it was readily practiced. White workers were paid more than Black ones and were given better benefits, positions, and representation. The boilermakers' union, for example, denied Black workers full membership, but because it had a closed-shop contract in the shipyards, the union still collected dues from the Black builders. Then, when hundreds of thousands of workers lost their jobs after the war, Black workers, often hired last, were fired first. With no ties to the area, and no experience in urban industrial work, many struggled to stay afloat. The benefits created by the federal government after the war—the home loans, college scholarships, and government jobs that together comprised arguably the largest public to private wealth transfer in American history—were largely denied to Black citizens.

Marin City was a town of about three thousand residents—

less than half the size of Sausalito—that, as mentioned, had been established in part to house the Black shipbuilders who, through redlining and exclusionary zoning ordinances, had been unable to secure housing in Sausalito. For example, southern Marin turned down a proposal to expand and update its water system because doing so would allow for the construction of new homes that would be available to Black workers. Limiting the housing stock kept real estate prices high, further stifling the ability of Black residents to own property. Though the two municipalities shared a zip code, the differences between them were stark: Sausalito was now less than 1 percent Black, whereas one-third of Marin City residents were Black, and Sausalito was 90 percent white, whereas Marin City was one-third white. The impact was felt not only on demographics but on resources. Despite being only twice the size of Marin City, Sausalito's operating revenue was over thirty times as large.

So how was it, Jeff wondered, that Marin City could support services for the unhoused, but Sausalito claimed to lack the resources?

"They have a community health clinic, they have housing, they accept Section 8. Sausalito does none of these things," Jeff shouted. "We can solve houselessness. We can do that now. We do that on the anchorage today—"

"Okay," said the mayor. "I'm gonna close public comment."

One council member joined Jeff in objecting to the letter, though for markedly different reasons: "I thought the letter didn't reflect all of the things Sausalito is doing and can do on this issue," she said. She asked that the letter be amended to include the work the city council had done in the previous few years to establish a zone at City Hall where an emergency shelter for twenty-three people could be built, even though the city had no plans to do so.

"Is everyone agreeable to that?" asked the mayor.

The council agreed.

"Okay, and so with those revisions . . ."

"So moved."

"That motion carries five to zero."

A few minutes later, comments were open again. Jeff marched back up to the podium to address the mayor. "Not one square inch of this earth was created by a man or a woman—"

"Jeff, please don't shout—"

"Every single square inch of this earth is God's property. That you"—he pointed at the council members—"are now representing a landlord in Washington, DC, named Donald J. Trump who has decided the country is his property—"

"Jeff, please don't shout—"

"—is an issue—"

"Thank you—"

"Not a penny for the houseless people. But $20 million for the people 'working' with them. They're called case managers." He turned to the sparse audience and warned them of God's plan for earth. "We are not allowed to use property as a profit center only. When there are people that do not have a place to lay their head, as Jesus and Elisha and Krishna and Buddha did not have a place, that in the East when they don't have any money, they're a renunciate, they are honored, they are given a robe of orange. People feel blessed when they come close to them. Here, now, it's a look, it's a feeling, it's a down-pression, that does not need to happen but is happening in the name of one thing and that thing is money."

Jeff stepped back from the podium, shouting now.

The mayor gave up trying to stop him.

"Sausalito was not settled by the monied people! It was settled by the sailors. The boats were here first. Every square inch now, on that hill, is a place coyotes can no longer be. Nor the mountain lions, nor a community garden, nor somebody living off the land, somebody fishing from a dock, nor somebody gathering wood for a cooking fire. When that is stamped out, for not just the hundred people out here, but for the eleven thousand people in this county, 71 percent who were born in Marin? That's *your* responsibility!"

He walked up close to the microphone again.

"Trump is a landlord now, and acting as one, for money interests around the country! If you are going to be a resistance to it, then *be one.*"

His timer beeped and he walked away.

14

RECEIVING LITTLE ASSISTANCE FROM THE CITY, THE ANCHOR-OUTS OFTEN relied on kind Sausalitans for help.

For years, each morning, a large white van stopped just outside Dunphy Park to take the anchor-outs for a hot meal at one of a few nearby churches. I joined them one Thursday a couple years earlier. The van was headed that day to Westminster Presbyterian Church, a few miles north in Tiburon.

There were maybe fifteen of us sitting on top of one another. Ten would have been too many. But a hot meal was not far off and spirits were high.

In front of me, a former ornithologist in a straw hat named Richard was recounting to his friend Sydney a history book he'd read about the Forty-Seven Ronin, a band of samurai who were left leaderless after their lord was forced to commit seppuku for assaulting a powerful provincial official. They rebelled against the court and killed the leader of the town, knowing that their lives would be taken in response.

"Yeah, Ronan," said Sydney, apparently only half listening to the details. "He was a lonely guy, no one to kill."

Richard, in the mood to talk, turned around in his seat to face me. "This has been a terrible year for sea lions," he said.

Oh?

"Yeah, all the baby sea lions have been starving to death. They think it's because of a few degrees of sea change. Similar to the starfish up in Washington. There are things the ocean understands but we don't. A marine biologist could say more. I'm more of a land guy. Of course, I spend a lot of time at sea."

WHEN WE PULLED UP AT THE church, the volunteers were still setting up lunch.

Some thirty anchor-outs had shown up and now were shuffling around the large all-purpose room, finding their seats at one of a half-dozen folding tables covered in flower-print vinyl. In the corner was a portable shelf from which anchor-outs could freely borrow as many books as they pleased. There I found Richard debating between three works: one, by Buckminster Fuller, explored the idea that technology was advancing in such a way that one could do "more and more with less and less until eventually you can do everything with nothing"; a second was about what he called "terrestrial climate change," something that was of great concern to him given the sea lion crisis; and a third, a detective novel by Agatha Christie. Eventually he selected the novel.

We were interrupted a few minutes later when a volunteer called everyone together to acknowledge some recent birthdays among the anchor-out regulars. Afterward, the foil was pulled off dishes of chicken, lasagna, ziti, meatballs, candied carrots, and peas. There were cupcakes too, and a bowl of rolls from which everyone filled their pockets. This was to be expected. The church provided Styrofoam to-go boxes so the anchor-outs could take back leftovers for their friends and loved ones who had missed the van or couldn't make the trip to Tiburon.

I sat down next to an anchor-out who was seated by himself, enjoying a few servings of chicken.

I asked him how his week was going.

He was in a sour mood, he said, locked in battle with California gulls, like Innate's Goofy and Broad, who were nesting on his boat. "The pigeons will nest on your boat too," he said, shaking his head. "They trash it in no time." He sighed and picked at his chicken. We finished our meals in silence.

During the meal, there was no prayer, no effort to proselytize; the anchor-outs, it was well known, had their own church, their own spiritual traditions. The pastor later told me that he could recall only one anchor-out joining Westminster as a result of the hot meals program. "He only stuck around for a year or two. He was kind of a drifter. I knew he was headed somewhere."

AFTER LUNCH, THE VAN DROVE US back to Dunphy Park and dropped us off near the remains of the *Galilee*.

I sat on the grass with Richard and Sydney.

I told Richard about the man at lunch who'd been so angry about the gulls nesting on his boat. Why not just let them? I asked.

"Because," he said, "you take off with their babies and you have to deal with the mother hunting you."

Richard began telling me about all the cormorants and pelicans and great blue herons and diving ducks that could be seen in Richardson Bay by just taking the time to stop and look out at the water. But a moment later, his attention was captured by a group of crows that landed on the mast of the *Galilee*.

"There's been a crow boom the last fifteen years," he said, clearly impressed.

Sydney nodded. When she was a girl, she said, there were none in Richardson Bay.

"Starlings came from New York. It took them a century to get here!"

Nearby, a group of anchor-outs sitting in the shade of a tree and splitting a container of leftovers had gotten ahold of a local paper. Their bellies full, everyone had been laughing and making plans on the ride back from Tiburon. But now it seemed that all the papers had to say about the group of men and women who had just returned from an afternoon celebrating one another's birthdays in church was that they polluted the bay, didn't pay taxes, brought crime to the waterfront, and lived miserable, drug-addled lives.

Richard looked over at the commotion and said, "Crows pop up increasingly onshore. They feed on other nests. It gets out of hand." Then he smiled: "Smartest birds in the world! They know how to exploit a niche."

He laughed, picked up his leftover chicken, and headed back to his boat.

Private assistance for the poor has always suffered from the uncertainties that accompany a fluctuating market economy. When the wealth gap is massive—as it is in Sausalito—this discrepancy is cast in sharp relief. In a community lacking the meaningful public assistance provided in a place like Marin City, the anchor-outs are vulnerable to the moral judgments of private residents, whose help is the only hope they have.

When people have less, they give less. For this reason, cities throughout most of the nineteenth century expanded their welfare programs as a way of addressing the poverty and homelessness that grew in the wake of the Industrial Revolution. However, that same industrialization gave rise to increasingly powerful companies that targeted poor relief, because federal and state assistance allowed working-class people to turn down the most dangerous and low-paying jobs. Corporations spent decades lobbying politicians to reduce public aid. They took aim especially at what was then called outdoor relief, which provided food, clothing, and money to unhoused and impoverished people without requiring them to be institutionalized. These companies instead funded the creation of private charity organization societies (COSs), which doled out relief based on their assessment of the moral worth of recipients. COSs deliberately framed poverty as a personal failure in an attempt to steer regulators away from establishing safety and minimum wage laws. So successful were they at dismantling the public welfare system that, in the last three decades of the nineteenth century, one-fourth of all US cities abolished welfare, while another 20 percent stopped offering financial outdoor relief. In all, 80 percent of cities cut back or canceled their public assistance programs. When this rollback began, only a few hundred people lived in Sausalito. With its low population, Sausalito never developed a robust public assistance program, despite the constant presence of a transient community on the anchorage throughout the twentieth century. This is how, once the population of the waterfront boomed in the 1960s and '70s, a former San Francisco brothel owner named Sally Stanford was able to win enough votes to become mayor simply by pledging to install public toilets.

IN DECEMBER 2018, I ARRIVED AT the police station, where I had made an appointment to discuss the claims I'd heard that the anchor-out population was increasing the crime rate in Sausalito. The front desk clerk informed me, however, that the department was too busy to answer any questions. Crime statistics, she said, were available online. Later, when I was unable to locate them, I filed a public records request with the Sausalito Police Department asking for "any available crime statistics for the anchor-out community." I never heard back.

After I left the station, I stopped by Smitty's. There the anchor-outs and Sausalitans often hung out and joked together as regulars.

Leaving their troubles in the outside world at the door, they laughed and shared a drink.

An anchor-out in a wide-brimmed hat was at the bar, telling a story to a group of Sausalitans about a wild skunk he'd recently adopted.

Everything was going well, he told the bartender, until a cat showed up on his boat. The skunk got spooked and sprayed the cat, and now the whole deck needed bleaching. Point was, he said, he was just trying to do a little good.

The bartender nodded.

A British guy laughed with his friend, who shortly after got up and left.

Everyone noticed that he didn't leave a tip.

The man apologized for his friend, explaining that he was from Canada.

The room looked confused.

"What is the difference between a Canadian and a canoe?" the guy said, by way of explanation.

What?

"A Canadian doesn't tip."

Next to me, someone who looked like a mariner began to laugh. I made a passing comment to him about the skunk hoping to strike up a conversation. He clocked me, as so often happened, as someone from out of town.

What was I doing there? he wondered.

I said I'd been trying to speak to the police about the anchorage, and the crime everyone so often mentioned in connection with the water.

Oh yes, he said. At one time he'd been an assistant harbormaster. He doubted I'd get much from the police, though; they weren't in the business of promoting crime spikes, he said. But he knew the water well. It was hard to keep track of who was out there, as so many didn't want to be found, he said. But several people a year were known to simply disappear. "Those you *don't* hear about," he said, sipping his beer.

But why the sudden concern about crime on the anchorage?

"The anchor-outs doubled in the last five years," he said, then explained that they came to Sausalito after the recent shuttering of the Redwood and Treasure Island anchorages and "the cleaning up of the Oakland estuary."

I'd heard the police cite these same closures on several occasions. But it was hard to imagine how closures alone accounted for a disproportionate increase in crime. After all, those who'd been living in other estuaries for years were more likely to be competent sailors than people grappling with addiction.

"Sure," he said. "You still have 10 to 15 percent of mariners, 30 percent who want to live off the radar."

I noted that most people I'd met who wanted to be off the grid tried to minimize their encounters with the law, not commit violent crimes that would be sure to draw scrutiny.

"Drugs and alcohol, meth, heroin, serious drug-related issues," he said. These things all contributed to the crime. Also, he added, "a huge percentage have mental health issues."

How did he know if someone had mental health issues?

"They're rowing with a two-by-four."

What about addiction?

"There are meth labs out there," he said. "Nowhere have I ever seen this. It's theft of services. The police don't cite. I don't know if I should be more mad at the police or the anchor-outs."

I told the man that his claim was not borne out by surveys of the unhoused in Marin County, more than two-thirds of whom fell into neither of those categories.

He shrugged. Maybe that was true, maybe it wasn't. But what was untenable, he said, was that the anchorage was growing, and its existence was representative of a "problem of society that is escalating." People were dropping out, they weren't paying their fair share, they wanted to live for free.

I pressed the former assistant harbormaster again on the idea that the talk of crime on the anchorage was overblown.

"Well," he said, "they are just mowing down the eelgrass. It's against the law."

So did he really think they should all be evicted?

He laughed. That would be chaos, he said. "If you really want to displace these people, you have to put them somewhere."

During my conversation, a guy with a full beard and a tall beer had been listening in. After the assistant harbormaster left, he introduced himself.

He had a big smile and lived on the hill.

He'd overheard my conversation, he told me.

I asked him what he thought about what had been said.

The former assistant harbormaster wasn't entirely wrong, he told me. The post–Great Recession years had brought to the anchorage more people living in desperation. And many of them did suffer from addictions and traumas. And it was true, it seemed, that an increase in this type of population had led to at least some increase in crime. But these problems were found in any community, including the neighborhoods on the hill. The solution, he said, was not to evict everyone, but to try to help people: love thy neighbor, as the Man says.

I hung around for a while longer.

He started mumbling something about how Jesus had a brother named Isukiri who took his place on the cross at Golgotha. Then Jesus had apparently headed east, through Siberia, to northern Japan, where he died at the age of one hundred in the village of Shingo.

He took a long sip from his glass.

In Japan?

He gave me a knowing look and said that some Christians believe that's where Jesus is buried.

I asked him what he did for a living.

"An unemployed full-time alcoholic."

PART 3

THE WIND ON THE WATER

2019–2020

15

AN UNEASY CALM HUNG OVER THE WATER THROUGH THE START OF 2019.
Sausalito had left the Richardson Bay Regional Agency, and its police officers, who had spent eighteen months citing, towing, and crushing boats, reported progress: only forty-five anchor-out vessels remained within the city limits, an almost 40 percent reduction. At meeting after meeting, the council members all agreed: a new era had begun.

The RBRA, meanwhile, was less enthusiastic. They counted 196 boats in their jurisdiction, a considerable increase from previous years. Combined with Sausalito, the total number in the anchorage was now 240, as high as it had ever been. In the end, Sausalito had spent hundreds of thousands of dollars in grants and budget allocations to harass and compel a small number of live-aboards to pick up anchor and move out a few hundred feet into RBRA-controlled waters.

The ironies were traded like jokes in Richardson Bay: Sausalito residents cited the anchor-outs' failure to pay taxes as justification for spending taxpayer dollars to push the community *out* of their taxable waters; they cited the damage to eelgrass on the bay floor from the dragging of anchors as the reason for forcing anchor-outs' boats to move to deeper waters, where their anchors dragged *more* severely; they cited the obstruction that floating homes presented to navigable waters to justify pushing them *closer* to the channel. As Jeff and Keven were as keen to point out at city council and RBRA meetings as they had been on park benches and Pirate Church gatherings, the only thing to disappear in this venture was public funds.

Not all anchor-outs wanted off the water. But some did, if only they had somewhere else to go. The police liked to say that they were "empowering anchor-outs toward an independent life," yet no money was used to build the twenty-three-bed homeless shelter the city so highly praised itself for finally incorporating into its zoning.

For the anchor-outs pushed farther out into the bay, day-to-day life had worsened: rowing to shore was more grueling, and the storms were more violent. Anchors dragged, lines crossed, hulls punctured. In an emergency, help was harder to come by. But living on the estuary was still manageable, endurable. Peace, with Sausalito, with the RBRA, had always been the goal. If this was the price, so be it.

THIS WAS THE MOOD ON THE estuary to which a mariner named Jim arrived in the fall of 2019. Jim was in his fifties, and ten years prior, he'd lived in Richardson Bay alongside Innate, Larry, and Bo. Back then, it was a peaceful place. He needed that again, to collect himself after a divorce on the East Coast had upended his life and business.

After his marriage ended, Jim had been living on a lake in Ithaca, New York, where he operated Airbnbs on two boats. College kids rented them for drunken weekends, and their parents rented them for graduations. It was a good, steady business, until a storm blew through that destroyed the vessels. Deciding he was finished with New York, he charted a course to sail the world. He'd saved enough money to buy a new boat and found some options in the Bay Area. So, like many in his situation, Jim boarded an Amtrak train, the *California Zephyr*, with the last of his belongings and headed toward his new life.

What Jim thought on that train, I'll never know. But a decade earlier, in 2010, I'd taken that same train when I moved to San

Francisco and first heard about the anchor-outs. His search for peace of mind, for distance from his mistakes and the mistakes of others around him, reminded me of many of my fellow passengers on that ride.

THOSE OF US MAKING THE THREE-DAY trip congregated in the observation car, joining a group of photographers who were hunched over their cameras as they calibrated their lenses. We shared stories of the railmen of the nineteenth century who first blew and bridged their way through the Sierras, cutting the path we'd soon travel. Unshowered and with film on our teeth, we got to know one another. We drank too much and played cards together at the small Formica tables. Our circumstances seemed to demand it as we shared our hopes for our unknown futures.

In Iowa, a woman in her sixties boarded the train. After playing a few hands, we went downstairs to the empty bar car and sat at a booth as the Great Plains settled into darkness. The smell of smoke filled the room, the wake of two old men in cowboy hats who were always moving about the lower deck sneaking cigarettes.

I asked her where she was headed.

Denver, she said. Many years ago, her daughter had stopped speaking to her and moved out west. But word had made it back to her in Mississippi that now her child was married and about to have a baby. She was sad but optimistic. She might never get another chance to be a good mother, but maybe things would still work out for her as a grandmother.

I looked out the window. It was now completely black. I told her it was a shame we couldn't see the long irrigation sprinklers snaking across the green Nebraska farms.

Not really, she said. A porter once told her that Amtrak

scheduled the stops and departure times along the route so that the train would pass through Nebraska at night. The photographers, who were frequent travelers on the underbooked *Zephyr*, found the state of little visual interest.

We sat in silence as the train wheels clacked beneath our feet. It occurred to me that the woman must have had that conversation with the porter on a previous trip to Denver.

At the woman's stop in Colorado, a man in his early twenties with a hiking backpack boarded the train. He asked those of us in the observation car if anyone was checking IDs against the names on tickets.

Sometimes, I said. But not for most people.

He nodded, taking in the risk. There was a warrant for his arrest, he said. So he was heading to Sacramento to start over. And he'd heard Sacramento was a big place.

That night, we all slept in our seats. By the time I entered the observation car the next morning, the regulars were already busy with their distractions. A woman whom I'd gotten to know the previous afternoon sat next to me, twisting a Rubik's Cube. She told me she'd heard a rumor that the lady sitting by the window playing guitar was a Kuwaiti pop star on a train tour of America. The day before, I'd seen the singer making out with the guy next to her. Already he looked heartbroken. She would be traveling all the way to Los Angeles. His last stop was San Francisco, which must suddenly have felt like a tragedy; he'd found what he was looking for too soon.

A woman in the lounge who smelled like vanilla began offering massages.

The porter laughed. This was nothing, he said. On the *Coast Starlight* line, which ran down along the edge of the Pacific, he once opened the door to an orgy in the baggage compartment. He shook his head. It was the strangest thing, that train: people just rode it back and forth, drinking and sleeping with strangers.

Everyone settled on hand-oil treatments.

I asked her why she was going to California.

She said she was starting a new life. Though she had just completed a massage therapy course in Oklahoma, she decided instead to move to San Francisco in the hopes of getting a job at the Lusty Lady, a peep show theater co-owned by sex workers.

Did she have any contacts there?

No, she said. But she'd find a way.

When at last our train pulled into Emeryville, from which I would catch the bus across the bay to San Francisco, the masseuse wrote down everyone's email address, saying she would check in at some point in the future and ask what each of us found in California.

It would have been hard for me to imagine, on that train in 2010, what my answer to that question would end up looking like. Only a few weeks after I disembarked the *Zephyr* and my bus dropped me off at the Embarcadero, I would hear of the anchor-outs for the first time. Over the years, as they'd tell me the stories of how they found themselves in poverty, floating in abandoned vessels in Richardson Bay, I'd often be reminded of one or another passenger I'd met on the *Zephyr*. Some were seeking an end to an aimless time in their lives, others a beginning. Each wanted to settle something in the past and finally turn things around. In California, as a friend of mine used to say, "*everything* grows."

On the Emeryville platform, the pop singer and the guy she'd met were hugging. He was crying as he begged her not to get on the *Coast Starlight* line.

Strange, I thought. Why didn't he just go with her? He'd boarded the train in search of a new life, and here it was. Maybe he wanted to be true to the person he was when he'd dreamed of that fresh start in San Francisco. Or maybe he already knew: he could get off now or get off later; most things don't work out.

WHEN JIM REACHED SAN FRANCISCO, HE had little but his boat money in his pocket. So he began couch surfing. In exchange for a roof over his head, he offered sailing trips once he got his vessel.

"One night I stayed at a woman named Tola's house," he explained. "The second night I told her about my two kids I hadn't seen in twenty years—it was a Thursday—and she said on Saturday, "I will see my kids for the first time in thirty years." He cherished the prospect. After he found a wooden sailboat to buy, he called her up and said, "I hope you don't mind, but I want to name my boat *Tola*, out of respect for people who deal with parental alienation."

She agreed.

Jim went to work patching up the *Tola Levine*. To get the craft seaworthy for the long voyage, he needed more than he could afford: a new wooden rudder, plus updated navigation equipment. So he went to work. He bought a secondhand bike and secured a position at a Peet's Coffee. He found odd jobs fixing up the old home of a woman a few towns north named Lisa. He steadied her doors on their hinges, scraped the flaking paint from her soffits, and before long they were dating.

Anchored in Richardson Bay, he put his life back together.

"It felt really good," he said.

A port in the storm was all he needed. In the days when William Richardson sold Sausalito spring water and whale blubber to passing sailors, this had always been the purpose of the anchorage: to serve as a place to stop and rest from harsh seas, to regroup. Their critics suggest that anchor-outs never leave, but surveys indicate that most remain only a few years.

Jim reconnected with familiar faces. There was Jeff, Dream, Doug. "I was like, wow, it's good to be back."

Soon, however, he noticed that no new mariners were arriving.

Unbeknownst to Jim, for about a year the RBRA and Sausalito had been working their way down a list of priorities for vessel removal. Having at this point rid the water of every boat that could plausibly be considered "marine debris," they had turned their attention to new arrivals. Clearing the anchorage was never universally popular in town, even among those who wished the anchor-outs gone. But the BCDC was demanding that all vessels be removed from the water by March of the following year.

One day, upon his return home after a long day of work at Lisa's house, Jim found a slip of paper taped to his cabin.

"I got a notice saying I had seventy-two hours to leave. I was like, 'What the hell?'"

16

AS JIM BEGAN HIS SEARCH FOR A NEW LIFE, INNATE AND MELISSA WERE finally settling into their home in the desert.

By the end of 2019, neighbors had begun dropping by, teaching them to work the alkaline soil. A horse rancher down the way who'd grown brittle with age gave Innate manure, asking that, in exchange, Innate spend some time with his animals. Melissa started helping a nearby woman shear her sheep; in return, the woman let her take some of the wool home to spin with a wheel that the woman's grandmother had gifted her. Another neighbor gave Melissa a slow cooker and jars, which she used to make marmalades and jams. All the while, they were adopting cats to defend their crops. Soon, those cats met a few other cats, who met a few more cats; before long Innate and Melissa were looking after more than twenty kittens. Again, neighbors helped them out, taking all but three of the animals off their hands. That left them with just as many cats as needed for the whole cycle to start again.

In time, as they became known around their patch of Arizona desert as "the sea hippies," their land slowly came to life. When a local named A-rod, who lived about twenty miles away, gave them rabbit pellets and coffee grounds for their garden, the almond and peach trees finally blossomed. In exchange, they traded fresh clean groundwater from their well. "After living on the bay and having to fight for water—with that hose flavor—you have no idea how happy it makes me to share my water with the neighbors," he told me on the phone one afternoon.

I asked Innate how life compared to the anchorage.

"I'm—*we're*—really doing way better than we were in Sausalito. People say, 'But it gets so windy out there.' Well, yeah! But the ground isn't moving."

Did it feel like the community they had in Richardson Bay?

Not really, Innate said. "We're small communities in pockets." Each person had so much land that they rarely crossed paths. There was the truck driver who lived in a storage container and hadn't been seen since his wife died. And there was the reclusive cattle rancher who stayed off the grid on two hundred solar-powered acres. Many residents of the desert were off the grid, of course, including Innate and Melissa. But those among them who had declared it a lifestyle were asserting their claim to solitude.

Innate was closest to A-rod.

A-rod had a prosthetic leg, and the two bonded when Innate began giving him rides to the hospital. Once, on the way home from such a trip, they stopped by the side of the road to smoke. They noticed a nearby oak tree and collected fallen acorns. On another hospital trip, as Innate waited for A-rod in the parking lot, he spotted aspen shoots across the street while walking his friend's dog. "I collected them up and stuck them in a water bottle," he said. In this way, the friends gradually amassed seeds and saplings of all sorts. They brought them back to Innate and Melissa's property, and together they all began planting them in the clay. Forty had taken root so far, Innate said. And soon, they hoped, they'd add ponderosa pines and white oaks and river birch trees, along with pussy, fall, grove, and weeping willows.

"The aspen is of the willow family," said Innate. He was especially fond of their aspen trees. Their roots, he explained, would one day all be interconnected: "If one dies, it can benefit from the others," he said. "I fucking love it."

As he continued to list trees and wonder about the animals they might attract to the property a century from now, Melissa called out into the phone: "All these trees that we are planting bring different nutrients to the property!"

"We're calling it N.M. Woods," Innate said.

Melissa laughed: "You wanna be N.M. Woods! Dontcha?"

Their tree grove, Innate hoped, would restore the land to what it had been long ago. "Most of the rocks you see are relics of broken trees," he said. "And I found one that I think is a dinosaur egg."

Melissa pointed out that even earlier, during the Paleozoic Era, the entire mesa they called home had been underwater, at the bottom of the sea. "But now," she joked, "*we've* become the Hill People."

"We're about a third the size of Sausalito."

I asked if they still spoke to anyone from their time on the anchorage.

"Once in a while," Innate said, "I'm able to get in touch with Dream." But they spoke less and less often as the years spent apart from one another began to accumulate; neither brother was very good at maintaining a phone number, let alone the phone itself. "Sometimes I wish I was closer." Still, Innate and Melissa never imagined returning to life on Richardson Bay. Out here, in the vast desert, the sky and the weather were something to behold, not to fear. "You can set your watch to the monsoons," he said. "They come at one or one thirty, done at three. It's really groovy, it's really an incredible scene, bolts of light connecting two regions of the sky—not even touching the ground. And we've got such an incredible view of the Milky Way. And it's truly beautiful, the pollution we get here."

Not long before we spoke, Innate and Melissa were in their grove, looking at the sky after a monsoon rain, when a triple rainbow appeared. Staring at it, his mind drifted back to when his life went sideways decades earlier, after the U-Haul containing his dog and everything he owned was stolen from the gas station in Rainbow, California. Looking up now, from the forty acres he owned with the partner he loved, where they would pass the rest of their days, he thought: "Wow, it's like a portal."

17

THE BAY CONSERVATION AND DEVELOPMENT COMMISSION'S MARCH 31
deadline for Sausalito and the Richardson Bay Regional Agency
to present a plan to evict the anchor-outs was fast approaching
when reports of a new coronavirus began to spread across the
country.

Little was known about the pathogen. The first laboratory-
confirmed case in the United States had been identified in mid-
January in Washington State. Two weeks later, the virus was found
in California. By March 17, fifteen cases had been identified in
Marin County alone, and a shelter-in-place order was issued. But
illness continued to spread. A week later, the number of cases had
more than doubled, and Sausalito announced that residents should
stay home at least until May 3.

The plan to clear the anchorage never materialized; the COVID-19
pandemic would quiet concerns about eelgrass decimation and channel navigability. To the anchor-outs' good fortune, $1 million in
funding was made available to help those who were most vulnerable
to infection. And police forsook their citation pads and began using
their patrols to identify unhoused residents in need of medical care.
In Dunphy Park, the city built mobile showers and passed out bags
of groceries.

Life nevertheless grew more difficult on the estuary, as many
of the anchor-outs lost their part-time work. Home renovations
were halted, coffee shops closed, and the need for domestic help
dried up.

In this time of upheaval, Jim lost the cash flow he needed to continue repairs on his boat. No matter, he thought, he would wait it out like everyone else. He'd received several temporary permits allowing him to stay. Once the pandemic was over, he would pick up work again and be on his way.

In July, however, Jim came home to another notice. "It said, 'If you don't leave, they will tow you away,'" he recalled.

But he couldn't leave. His boat, in which he'd invested thousands, still wasn't seaworthy. And with all his savings from Ithaca tied up in the vessel, he couldn't afford to lose it either. "In the last year they have destroyed several sailboats. Several boats that people have been living on, and so leaving them homeless. And so that's my concern."

LOCKDOWNS IN CALIFORNIA KEPT ME OFF the anchorage for most of the year.

When I arrived in Sausalito for the first time in the fall of 2020, the place was quiet. Ferry service had been reduced, and the last ride back to San Francisco, even on the weekends, was 6:00 p.m. The pigeons, accustomed to years of tourist traffic, now hopped around the town fountain with abandon.

Just off the ferry dock was the Hotel Sausalito, which was built in 1915. It had narrow halls and creaky stairs. The place felt empty. I wasn't sure who would be left on the water, so I decided to get a room.

I waited by the front desk until a man appeared. He explained that there were not enough guests to warrant being on duty full-time.

How had life been since the pandemic started? I asked.

He shrugged. "Some in town like the quiet."

When I went up to my room, the television didn't work and the clock on the wall was off by two hours.

THE NEXT MORNING I WALKED DOWN Bridgeway to the Taste of Rome coffee shop, where a few anchor-outs could reliably be found inside, their hiking backpacks piled in the corner, their flip-phone charger cords dangling from the outlets.

I ran into Doug on the back patio overlooking the estuary. The day was blue and breezy, but hardly anyone was walking around outside.

The pandemic lockdowns, I noted, seemed to calm eviction efforts.

Doug adjusted his sock hat. That was true for a little while, he said. But I'd be mistaken, he added, to assume that, in the long run, the coronavirus would improve the situation. "This whole thing in 2020, society has changed. The problem is, it has changed the nature of the anchorage. There is no doubt the economics forced people out there. It's their last hope."

The most desperate people are always the most despised.

Soon, Doug said, the city would realize that Richardson Bay was filling up with people who lost their homes and jobs in the lockdowns. They weren't seasoned sailors, and they didn't know how to fix a boat. Their needs and struggles would be visible to everyone onshore. When that happened, the war would start again, as it always had, at least since he arrived in 1987. "I'm a minister. I get here, and a week later Sausalito is contemplating getting rid of the anchor-outs. There is a spiritual aspect—just like when God chastises Israel."

Doug was referencing the Book of Kings, where the prophet Ahijah predicts the fall of Jeroboam, the first ruler of the northern Kingdom of Israel, who led the revolt against the Kingdom of Judah: "And the Lord will strike Israel, so that it will be like a reed swaying in the water. He will uproot Israel from this good land that he gave to their ancestors and scatter them beyond the Euphrates River, because," by worshiping the idols of another god, "they aroused the Lord's anger."

When did he think this would happen?

It already was happening, Doug said as he lit a cigarette.

A family eating next to us sighed.

Doug recounted what happened not long ago when his friend's boat drifted from RBRA territory into Sausalito waters. The police jumped on board, pulled her out, impounded her boat, and arrested her. They charged her with resisting arrest.

What happened to her boat?

They crushed it, he said. This, he feared, was the likely fate of another friend's boat that was recently impounded under similar circumstances. And need he even mention the case of an anchor-out named Kim? When the harbormaster boarded her boat without her permission, she confronted him with bear spray, not knowing who he was. She was arrested and jailed, though it was well known that women living alone on the anchorage were frequently forced to defend themselves from intruders. Her case has yet to go to trial.

I asked Doug what he made of it all.

"Shit rolls downhill." He took a drag of his cigarette.

The nearby family gathered their meal and moved to a faraway table.

Doug looked out across the patio to the 130 boats now left on the water. "I feel like Jeremiah, the weeping prophet."

What?

"This is happening."

THE FOLLOWING NIGHT IT RAINED. I walked with Jim and Lisa up the shore until we got to the dock where their dinghy was tied up.

As Jim began to fill water jugs from the pump, Doug pulled up in his pickup truck. He leaned out the window and called out to Jim.

Jim groaned.

It had been only a few weeks since Donald Trump lost the presidency to Joe Biden. Trump's myriad legal challenges, Doug said, were *sure* to overturn the election and make things right.

Jim peered up at the sky. Looked like more rain; he needed to get going.

Hold on, Doug said. He was driving around delivering brown-bag dinners for anyone in need of food. Did we want some?

Jim took two, and they parted ways.

As we walked back to the pump, I told Jim I was surprised Doug wanted Trump to be president.

These were strange times, Jim warned. But in some ways he understood: in Sausalito, only 12 percent of residents were registered Republicans. Many of the people creating the policies, applying the political pressure, and enforcing the eviction of the anchorage considered themselves liberals.

It sounded, I said, like the water had more Trump sympathizers than the hill.

Maybe, he said. But who knows what to make of that. It isn't as if the anchor-outs are following the news, hanging on every word or sentence of one or another politician in Washington, DC. Things had gotten pretty complicated since the pandemic started.

How so?

Out there, he said as he pointed into the misty darkness, a *lot* of people on the water didn't wear masks.

As we loaded the gallon jugs of water onto Jim's dinghy, he asked me if I wanted to spend the night on his boat.

I told him I did, if it was okay with Lisa.

She laughed. She had no plans to sleep on a boat tonight. It was best to stay out of the storms.

WHEN I WOKE UP ON THE *Tola Levine*, I walked out into the main cabin, where Jim had slept on a sleeping bag. The room was dark, with just a small light in the galley, where he was attempting to assemble a new hand-cranked coffee grinder. So many of the boats I'd been on creaked and moaned on the water. They smelled of sawdust and human juices. Jim's boat felt different; in another life, it might have had a slip at the sailing club.

He dropped the metal pieces of the grinder onto the counter and shook his head. A moment later he began pulling charts and maps from wooden cubbies built into the wall of the boat.

I asked him what he was doing.

He groaned, scolding himself: "If you are gonna know where one manual is, this is the one to know."

I tried to ask him about what it had been like living on the anchorage during the pandemic, but he was transfixed by the task of assembling the grinder. When, at last, he put it together, he placed some beans inside and gave it a crank. The dim yellow countertop light cast thick black frown lines across his face as he thumbed the grounds.

The grind was too coarse, he said. The coffee would be terrible. He'd lived for years in Nicaragua, and he knew what coffee was supposed to taste like. He disassembled the device again.

Why did he think Sausalito had become so hostile to the anchorage?

These sorts of things happen, he said. Once, while he was sailing in Nicaragua, he put his boat onshore to do some repairs. By the time he was ready to put it back in the water, the country had changed its anchoring policy. They charged him a 40 percent import tax on the vessel. When he couldn't pay, they seized his boat. With no way to leave, he simply stayed. He started a coconut oil business, transporting the goods from the western half of the country to the east. For years, as he saved for a new boat, coconut oil sustained him. He couldn't say enough about the benefits of coconuts.

"When you've got no choice, you just have to go along with things." He trailed off midsentence, consumed still by the grinder assembly.

I looked at the clock and suggested we settle for coarsely ground beans.

No, he said. The beans were a gift from the manager at Peet's. He wanted to prepare them properly. "It's getting better," he assured me. "I just have to fine-tune it more."

So why was he in Nicaragua to begin with?

"I was planning that trip since I was five. I was going to sail around the world."

I looked at the cabin walls. He had maritime charts of the coastlines from what seemed to be everywhere on earth. Locally, there was Drake's Bay and Golden Gate South to Santa Cruz. He'd stuck wooden pegs in the rolled-up ends of the San Francisco Bay and San Joaquin River maps, in case he ran up on some rocks and needed to hammer them into a leak. He knew where the channels were, knew how to calculate the right times in the tide cycle to traverse them. "All these guides show you safe places to anchor around the world." This was why Richardson Bay was established. If not for people seeking safe harbor, what were anchorages for? Yacht clubs? A pristine view for hilltop mansions? Much like Keven before him, Jim felt he had to resist his eviction, to protect the right of sailors to explore the earth. And, he said, he was nothing if not patient, nothing if not persistent. He could outlast anyone.

A smile came across his face. He ground the beans again. The consistency, he declared, was perfect. He put a kettle on the stove and brought it to a boil.

"This is the longest cup of coffee you have ever waited for."

I checked the clock again. The whole operation had taken more than an hour.

"It is for me too," he said, before taking a long, satisfying sip. He set a steaming steel mug in front of me.

The coffee was good, I told him.

He assured me it was far better than good. "I have some milk if you want it," he said as he unscrewed a jar of coconut milk and put a few spoonfuls into his cup. He sat down on the bench across from me and lost himself talking about a memory from his school days. "Once," he said, "I went on a hunger strike in detention. There is a part of me that is just that little kid."

As we drank our coffee, Jim pulled out the sack lunch Doug had given us the night before. In it was a turkey sandwich, some Fritos, and an orange. Jim started to peel the fruit.

I asked him what he thought Sausalito planned to do with the anchor-outs.

He brushed me off. "You can't control what happens to you in life." If you show up at the wrong time, he explained, things just don't go how you want them to. He asked if I had ever hitchhiked.

I hadn't.

"Well, I tried to hitchhike from Miami to Ithaca, New York. I found that the closer you got to DC, the harder it was. They emanate paranoia and fear from the capital."

Waves rolled below us.

The glasses on the counter shook as the unpeeled orange tumbled to the floor.

Jim laughed: "Now that's an example of a person who is going too fast." He took a bite of the turkey sandwich.

As we rocked back and forth Jim told me we would wait out the rough water on the boat, before making the twenty-minute row into shore. He wasn't due there until the evening, when he had seasonal work assembling grills at Home Depot.

"It's expensive to live in this area," he said. "A lot of people living out here are on the verge of homelessness. If they kick them out, that's what they'll be."

18

JIM DROPPED ME OFF AT THE DOCK BEFORE DISAPPEARING ON HIS BICYCLE up Bridgeway. The sky was gray and brooding. The anchor-outs milling about onshore were uneasy.

As I soon learned, sometime while Jim and I were asleep, a fire had broken out on the anchorage, on the boat of a sixty-seven-year-old man named Halsey. He was anchored just a couple hundred yards off the coast by the Army Corps of Engineers headquarters, where many of the seized boats of the past few years had been crushed.

First responders had arrived almost immediately after the fire started. But they were too late. Just after midnight, Halsey was pronounced dead.

Information about what exactly had happened traveled slower on the waterfront than the news of the blaze itself. Everyone in town saw what they were looking for: proof that the residents didn't have the training to handle emergencies on the water. They saw the fire as evidence that the boats themselves were a danger to their occupants, another example of the anchorage violence believed to be so commonplace and brutal.

Jeff did his best to quell suspicions. There were generators on the boat, he told a reporter at the *Marin Independent Journal*. The generator on Halsey's boat must have exploded. "He was a seaworthy sailor," Jeff said. "He knew what he was doing out there. It could have happened to any boat."

A FEW NIGHTS LATER, THE ANCHOR-OUTS gathered for Pirate Church on the concrete patio outside City Hall.

The minister, an anchor-out in his seventies, named Peter, who had been living on the anchorage for decades, was sitting at a picnic table holding a bottle of Jack Daniels. Behind him was a homemade sign that read PEOPLE ARE NOT DEBRIS. Peter preached God's word of love for the poor, railed against the "limousine liberals" trying to evict the anchor-outs, and took photographs of the sky when he believed the clouds contained a vision of Christ. Next to him, a man was playing the guitar over the sound of one anchor-out yelling at another for bringing his dog to church.

I spotted Jeff with Dream at the far end of the patio, next to a slow cooker filled with pulled pork. Dream, dressed in a windbreaker, was sitting in a wheelchair. I hadn't seen him since the pandemic started.

I hope you are okay, I said. Did something happen?

He laughed at me while he smoked a cigarette. "I'm good, man!"

I noted all the whispers around us about Halsey. How his death might not have been an accident.

Jeff shook his head at me, disappointed that I was putting so much weight on the rumors.

"They're grieving," he said, imploring me not to judge and take literally everything I heard.

Within a few more minutes, maybe twenty people had arrived. A handful of anchor-outs, led by a woman wearing costume wings, stood in a line crying as they shouted their memories of Halsey: how he was a good guy, always helping a neighbor in the storm. Someone walked around with the whiskey, filling everyone's cups.

Jeff stood up with a worn-out copy of the Hebrew Bible and began reading from the Book of Isaiah: "The spirit of the Lord God is upon me!" he shouted, "because the Lord hath anointed me to bring good tidings unto the humble; He hath sent me to bind up the broken-hearted, to proclaim liberty to the captives, and the opening of the eyes to them that are bound; To proclaim the year of the Lord's good pleasure, and the day of vengeance of our God; to comfort all that mourn . . ."

I sat down next to a bearded old man wearing a pirate hat.

Lotus, an anchor-out I'd known since 2015, put her hand on my back and introduced the man as Daniel Egginck.

He smiled at me and ran his fingers through his long sandy-white hair. "I'm an eighty-two-year-old California veteran, 129 Air East Supply Squad. They were wiped out in Vietnam, but I was not with them."

Daniel had been in the Bay Area as long as anyone out on the water. By his reckoning, he had started the whole thing: "*The Oracle*," he said, "was a left-wing rag going nowhere. I'm the last living member of *The Oracle*."

I hadn't heard of it, I said.

The San Francisco Oracle, he explained, was a short-lived but influential magazine on the Haight-Ashbury scene between 1966 and 1968. Perhaps its best-known issue was number 7, which included what is known as "The Houseboat Summit," a discussion held on Watts and Varda's *Vallejo*, in which Watts, Allen Ginsberg, Timothy Leary, and Gary Snyder debated the question: Drop out or take over? Snyder argued in favor of dropping out, the path traveled by many of the older anchor-outs like Larry, Daniel, and Peter: "Human beings want reality. That's, I think, part of human nature. And television, and drinking beer, and watching television, is what the working man laid off does for the first two weeks. But then, in the third week, he begins to get bored, and in the fourth week he wants to do something with his body and his mind and his senses." Drop out for long enough, and you will discover a new, more satisfying way to live.

Daniel laughed at the memory. "We launched the Summer of Love. From there? I was the man."

I didn't know much about it, I said.

"Oh yeah," he said. "It was Ginsberg's idea that we stone the Hells Angels"—a reference to the time when Ginsberg, Ken Kesey, and Hunter S. Thompson dosed the biker gang. "I had three years dosing LSD when there was no law against it." He pointed up at the hill. "There are thousands of people still in Marin County who I dosed."

Still?

Yeah, he explained. A lot of older Marin residents, to one degree or another, were once a part of the Haight-Ashbury scene, the Summer of Love scene, the houseboat scene. But they moved on after the Houseboat Wars, perhaps first financially and then ideologically, to make their money in the boom times of the eighties and the dotcom era of the late nineties. "What I have learned is: every community has a Judas."

I asked who the anchor-out Judas was.

"Hard to pin down. Every Judas has been a real estate dealer."

At one point, Lotus put her hand on Daniel's shoulder. "He brought Larry Moyer here," she said.

I was sorry to hear when Larry died.

"They were all contracted by the CIA."

What exactly he was talking about, I wasn't sure. But the mention of the CIA reminded me of a time, five years before, when I was on Larry's boat and he gave me what he said was the contact information for Oleg Gordievsky, a former KGB colonel who defected to the United Kingdom in 1974 and began working as a double agent for MI6. "He can confirm everything," Larry had said. I'd written to Gordievsky but never received a reply.

I asked Daniel if he had any idea what Larry might have been talking about.

"Larry was bringing cocaine in," he said. "All of them were contract agents."

Just then, an anchor-out walked up to Daniel and placed a bag of weed on the Bible sitting on the table in front of him. As Daniel began to sift through it, a young woman approached who seemed anxious to meet him.

"My name is Angel," she said.

"I like to be called Brother Daniel."

She sat down at our table, joining Lotus and a man in a camouflage baseball cap who, unprompted, repeatedly stated that he would not reveal his name.

Everyone seemed to be waiting for Daniel to speak as he picked at the buds. Finally he said: "I am convinced Jesus Christ is outraged by our conduct. What happened in Japan was extinction."

Daniel and the man in the camouflage cap began discussing the Fukushima nuclear disaster in 2011, when the most powerful earthquake ever recorded in Japan created a tsunami that crashed into the Fukushima Daiichi Nuclear Power Plant, leading to reactor core meltdowns after the plant lost power.

"I don't think people realize the world has ended," the man in the cap said.

As the man and Daniel spoke with one another, I couldn't help but think about why he might have chosen the Fukushima disaster as the end of the world. There had been many previous nuclear disasters. But 2011 was just after the Great Recession and just before the anchorage swelled and Sausalito and the RBRA began their crackdown. Their world *was* ending in 2011.

I looked over at Jeff, who was standing on a bench, reading the word of God to a group huddled together in the cold eating pulled pork sandwiches.

"There are big-time disasters coming," said Daniel. "It has already started."

"We are doomed."

"Yes."

"These are the times in the Book of Ezekiel!"

Before the end times, it is predicted in the Book of Ezekiel, God will create a great earthquake, followed by floods and fire, and

establish a new temple. The story is referenced in the Book of Revelation, which had gained some notoriety on the anchorage among
a group who believed that the COVID vaccine was the Mark of the
Beast. Daniel, like many Christian scholars, interpreted the Mark
as belonging to the Antichrist, or to a false god worshiped by fools.
As he saw it, only those with the Mark were permitted to enjoy the
niceties of American life: restaurants, libraries, buses, hospitals. "No
one can buy or sell unless he has the Mark, that is, the name of the
beast or the number of its name," Revelation says. "This calls for
wisdom: let the one who has understanding calculate the number
of the beast."

"I'm an old man," Daniel said. "I'm here to say the Mark of the
Beast is real."

The man in the cap leaned toward me. He told me to remove
my face mask.

I refused.

Did I have any idea what I was supporting? he asked. Not long
ago, the US Navy deployed what they were calling a "hospital ship"
to deal with coronavirus patients in California. Soon everyone would
be sick, and there would be no way for an unhoused person to get
a doctor but to board one of these ships. Down on Fourth Street in
San Rafael, at the encampment underneath the Highway 101 overpass, there were already whispers of residents being led out of their
tents and onto buses. Once all the unhoused were on board, the boat
would sail off into the Pacific, never to be seen again.

It sounded like a conspiracy theory, I told him.

He put his hat on the table, growing angrier. All these years
I'd been coming out here—was I blind? he asked. Of *course* there
was a conspiracy to get rid of the poor. All I had to do was go right
through those glass doors behind us, to any city council meeting.
The past few years had been one big plot against the unhoused
and the anchor-outs in Sausalito. In 2016, there were 240 boats in
Richardson Bay. Now there was what? Maybe 90. Where did all

those people go? He threw up his hands and shouted into the sky: "I am sure we are going to experience a serious disaster!"

I apologized and told him he was right. Somehow, it appeared, the city and the RBRA had used COVID as an excuse or a distraction or an opportunity to clear the water of anchor-outs. We might disagree on the details, but he was correct about the outcome: the community was being destroyed. And where did all those people go? Not onto military vessels that sailed off into the Pacific, surely. But somewhere.

Daniel leaned in between us, smiling. "The existing powers have done us wrong," he said. "The mortgage schemes, the evictions. Taking away our children. Taking away our health."

I pulled down my mask.

It was nighttime now, and the breeze was picking up.

Daniel put his hand on my back. "You were not getting any of that wholesome air."

WHEN THE TIME CAME FOR ME to leave, I walked down the path toward the water. Angel caught up to me and stopped me by the jungle gym.

There was something she wanted to be sure I understood.

What was that?

"I don't *want* to be an anchor-out," she said. Only last year she was making $76,000. But she'd lost her home. And now she had no choice.

I asked her why she went to the anchorage.

"It's really hard to live on a boat. But it feels a lot safer than being on San Francisco's streets. It's like a catch-22."

She had a job working in a restaurant, and she hoped to rent an apartment. "I want to go back to the community," she said. But she felt like she'd been forgotten about. "It's like they threw us away and don't care. They yell at us for trying to get *water*."

Around town, I told her, it wasn't hard to find a sympathetic ear. While the politicians talked mostly about eelgrass, the residents, at least to me, seemed to feel bad, but they were also under the impression that the community brought crime to the town.

"There are sickos in any community," she said.

Over the years, I'd heard stories from women who lived alone on the water about their boats being sabotaged by men who didn't approve of their independent lifestyles. And then there were the tales of the scorned former boyfriends who would steal their ex-partners' skiffs and hold them hostage at sea.

But, Angel wondered, were these reasons to destroy the anchor-out community? Why weren't they entitled to the same protections that a resident on land would receive? Surely, if a woman was held hostage in her home on the hillside, the solution wouldn't be to bulldoze her neighborhood? No. In fact they might *still* blame the anchor-outs. As Jeff had pointed out a year earlier to the city council, some of the crimes attributed to unhoused people and anchor-outs, like the man who killed his landlord, were actually committed by people with homes. At times the conventional wisdom seemed to be not only that being an anchor-out made you a criminal, but that being a criminal made you an anchor-out. Anyway, Angel said, much of what the town did seemed criminal to her. "My boat caught on fire. They crushed it. There is no place to get water, no place to throw out our trash." She still worked in Sausalito, but it felt as if the residents had exiled her. "I will probably serve them at my restaurant."

19

IN EARLY DECEMBER, BOTH OF JIM'S EYES GOT INFECTED. UNABLE TO SEE, he had no choice but to leave his boat and check himself into the hospital.

A few days later, word reached him from the anchorage: the harbormaster had taken the *Tola Levine* to the debris yard at the Army Corps of Engineers, where many of the anchored-out vessels deemed inoperative were crushed.

At the time, Jim was unable to leave the hospital. He had invested $200,000 in his boat, a 1962 De Dood International, as he made repairs on it. As Jim discovered, the harbormaster was claiming that his boat had drifted into the channel, making it a significant navigational issue for vessels entering and leaving the bay. He was told that, while he was gone, there was a "wind event" that moved the *Tola Levine* into harm's way.

"What the hell is a 'wind event'?" Jim said, recounting the day. To him, the timing felt off. He first started hearing about this more than a month ago. Only now, when he was in the hospital and unable to respond, was his boat moved?

"If it's such a dangerous situation, why did it take him five weeks to move my boat?"

But was he blocking the channel?

"No! I have witnesses that say, 'No, your boat was not in the channel.'"

The harbormaster disputed this claim in the local press. "The boat was at the edge of the channel," he told the *Pacific Sun*. "In the channel, honestly. I kept on getting complaints from the Coast Guard and the Army Corps of Engineers. It was a navigational hazard, especially at nighttime. Unacceptable."

The harbormaster threatened publicly to "dispose of" the *Tola Levine*. Meanwhile, a local activist named Robbie, who became an anchor-out to avoid exposing his father to the coronavirus, gathered a group of anchor-outs to occupy Jim's boat in protest. Dating back to the days of the Houseboat Wars, it was well understood that, without a legal fund, the best way to save a boat from destruction was to stay on it. And so, with chains and locks, they bound themselves to the vessel. The standoff lasted for five days, until the harbormaster agreed to tow Jim's boat up through San Pablo Bay and into the Napa River to a slip at the Vallejo Yacht Club, where Jim could carry out his repairs. Having no choice, Jim agreed. In return, he was banished from living on Richardson Bay.

"I just want to be. At some point you just don't have time for all that bullshit. That's the way the government works. If they are after someone, or after a group, they make it so time-consuming that you have to either have an unlimited budget for legal fees or deal with it on your own, but they just keep going and going and going."

A WEEK AFTER JIM WAS EVICTED from the water, I showed up at Pirate Church outside the library, hoping to see him there. The crowd was smaller, worn down. Daniel told me that he'd been spending more time under the 101 overpass in San Rafael. Since the pandemic, the encampment had steadily grown as evictions continued. Because the land beneath the overpass was state-owned, unhoused residents had been able to put together a tent city out of reach of local officials. It was only one of many encampments that had cropped up in Northern California since the pandemic began. The state's unhoused population had increased to such a degree that, even filled to maximum capacity, shelters could house only about 30 percent of those in need of a roof and a hot meal.

Jim never showed up at church; I was told that he'd stopped coming to Sausalito. Days later, I found him farther up the bay. He and Lisa and I ate one night at a dockside restaurant, where he told me that he was done with the anchor-out fight. With three jobs now—working at Peet's and Home Depot and teaching chess to kids—there just wasn't time. But even his short stay on the anchorage had given him something: he had paid off $40,000 in debt and now had enough money to raise the *Tola Levine* out of the water and finish his repairs. Once he could build a new rudder and get it steering, he'd be out to sea once more.

As church ended that night, more people than usual hung around.

I saw a woman I'd spoken to before. She looked exhausted, almost afraid of everyone. She didn't want me to use her name.

A few weeks before, she'd felt that the town had fully turned against her. "They won't even open up bathrooms," she had said. "There is no place in all of Sausalito. In America, people are raised to be proper about it, or whatever. Well, I think a lot of people who are unhoused—if they could bathe every day . . ."

I thought back to years ago, when Innate was preoccupied with trying to build his own shower. Rose too.

"When a gym found out I was living on the water, they wouldn't renew me for the next month." All that was left for them to use was the public restroom by the private tennis courts, where Sausalitans spent their summers enjoying the view of Richardson Bay. "It's this big huge concrete building. It's so utilitarian. There are no mirrors. It's just a big sheet of metal. It's a facility that's large enough that you could put showers in there. Why not? You want to think that people are good, but then . . ."

Sitting alone at the end of a picnic table, she smiled at me in a way that said she was no longer of the impression that talking about it would make any difference.

I ran into Jeff as I was leaving.

Jeff was always skeptical of me when he saw me hanging around. Journalists often seemed to side with the Hill People. But he knew I sometimes needed a place to sleep, especially when the ferry stopped running for the night, so he offered me a spot on his boat.

For a change, I asked him if he wanted to crash with me instead, at the Hotel Sausalito, where I was staying.

THAT NIGHT JEFF AND I ATE samosas and watched television. In the morning, he told me he was writing a story about an anchorage. But he was doing it as fiction, set in the nineteenth century in Charleston, South Carolina.

I asked him if the story was about the anchor-outs.

Of course, he said. The anchor-outs are part of a long tradition, going back centuries and more. There have always been communities on the water. It was an old story. It began with the Coast Miwok people who lived along the shore and later traded with Richardson. The anchor-outs were part of that lineage.

He let me read a few pages.

I asked if I could see more.

No, he told me. The end was yet to be written.

20

BY THE END OF 2020, DOUG WAS LIVING OUT OF HIS TRUCK. ITS TRUNK WAS packed with blankets, clothes, diving gear, and plastic tubs holding a lifetime of records about his scuba-diving business, his legal issues with the RBRA, and his plan for a mooring field on the anchorage. He'd been trying for years to engineer a resolution to the troubles on the estuary. Installing a mooring field, where permanent anchors are buried deep in the seafloor, would stop the destruction of the eelgrass and allow anchor-outs to keep their homes. He always found some receptive mariners and a few interested people on the city council or in the RBRA, but his proposal never went anywhere. The issue, as he saw it, was that no one could agree on what problem they were solving. Many in town rejected his idea not because it was a bad solution, but because it would allow the anchor-outs to stay on permanently. Some anchor-outs, meanwhile, felt that the installation of mooring fields would make their housing situation even *more* precarious. They figured that if mooring fields were added, they would be sold off to wealthy boat owners in a matter of years. All one had to do was look at the waterfront: they demolished most of the original community and replaced it with million-dollar floating homes. Anyone who went along with that, as Daniel would say, was just another Judas.

Doug's living situation had endowed him with a newfound sense of impermanence, so I was helping him digitize his records to store them in "the cloud," as he put it. One afternoon, I was returning a tub to him in a gravel parking lot downtown and noticed that he looked particularly grief-stricken.

I asked him what was wrong.

"The anchor-outs, coronavirus, the BCDC. It's like the Euphrates and the Tigris coming together. No man knows the hour or the day, but the generations will know." He looked up to the clouds and moaned.

What would they know? I asked.

"We're living in the apocalypse," he said, shoving the bin full of mooring field plans into the truck. "The sky was orange—remember that?"

Yes, I said. The orange sky was smoke and air pollution from a wildfire.

"I mean *physically* you could describe it as: 'there was a marine layer and the smoke sat on top of it. And the sky turned orange,' but . . ."

I gave him a confused look.

"I think people are asking questions. In the midst of all this, they want answers. What does God think? Someone can come along and take their anchor, their moorings. Like the Book of Judges, the question is: Who will God lift up? There is something going on here. Like when you are sailing and you see the wind on the water. It's coming."

I leaned in to help him shift his possessions around as he tried to close the trunk.

He turned to me: "I hope the anchor-outs start following Jesus, instead of following their own way. Because that doesn't end well. Just ask Jonah, who got himself swallowed by a whale." He would try to help them. He had planned to start up his denomination of the Pirate Church again, to teach anyone willing to listen. "That's why I left Peter. People weren't taking it seriously. People were nutting up. So I'll hold court like Paul, in the gazebo at Dunphy Park."

He slammed the trunk shut and wiped his hands on his pants.

I asked him how he thought things would end.

"Now, I'm just a representative of God," he said, then began to quote from the Epistle to the Hebrews, a book of the New Testament that some believe to have been written by Paul: "'We have this hope as an anchor for the soul, firm and secure. It enters the inner sanctuary behind the curtain . . .'"

The verse from Hebrews encouraged Jewish Christians to persevere in their belief that Jesus was the Messiah, despite their persecution.

"Does it apply now? Are these myths? Are these fables? Translations of translations?"

PART 4

THE STORM
2021–2022

21

AS THE PANDEMIC SPREAD THROUGHOUT 2020, HOMELESSNESS IN CALI-
fornia increased by about 6 percent. People desperate for shelter
were drifting onto the anchorage. In the years prior to Sausalito's
crackdown on live-aboards, the anchor-outs had taken in many of
those who came to town without a place to stay. But now, with more
unhoused people in need of beds, there were fewer empty boats to
spare.

A few weeks before the end of 2020, Daniel made his way to a
patch of tall grass and palm trees at the southernmost edge of Dunphy Park and pitched a tent in a fennel field. Here would be a place
of refuge, for both those evicted from the water and for the newly
unhoused residents of Marin County. It was a big blue tent with a
tarp stretched over the top to keep the rain away. Daniel named it
"Sanctuary."

The property where he erected the tent had gone unused for
decades, ever since the police station that once stood there was
demolished. Bo believed that it was the site of an ancient burial
ground, but all that was known for certain to be buried there was
tons of lead-contaminated soil.

For a few days, it was just Daniel occupying the tent. But soon,
anchor-outs who'd had their boats crushed by the RBRA began
showing up. The continued dispossession of vessels during the pandemic was, in the agency's eyes, an unfortunate necessity. A year
earlier, the state of California had audited the BCDC and concluded
that the commission had failed "to perform key responsibilities" and

had "allowed ongoing harm to the San Francisco Bay." A mandate to evict the anchor-outs was then passed to the RBRA, whose new harbormaster was tasked with enforcing it. He described the agency as being "as mom-and-pop as you can get," but said that it would nevertheless begin to move toward the removal of all anchored vessels. The policy, known as the "Transition Plan," rapidly increased the number of seizures.

Though the harbormaster maintained that he never crushed anyone's primary residence, the camp continued to grow. For a month or so, the city seemed to tolerate the small outpost. But when a winter storm blew across the water in late January, with wind gusts above sixty miles an hour, twenty-three vessels broke loose. Boats on the anchorage, sometimes held in place by as little as an old fender or engine block, were particularly vulnerable. Waves washed a handful of them into marinas and onto the shore, in some cases destroying them, or at least making them temporarily unseaworthy.

Those who lost their homes began to join Daniel, and slowly the camp grew. By early February, it housed around a dozen people, many of them elderly and in one or another way disabled; for them, life on the water would have been far too taxing. Many other names for Sanctuary emerged onshore and in the dwindling anchorage: Camp Jesus, Camp Unity, and Camp Rainbow Bay. The last was a reference to the alternative name that Daniel and some of the other anchor-outs had given Richardson Bay in recognition of the fact that it and Sausalito should never have been taken in the first place from the Coast Miwok and given by the Mexican government to William Richardson. Eventually, the name that stuck was Camp Cormorant. They drew white cormorants on rainbow Pride flags and hoisted them up on PVC flagpoles planted in the dirt.

Many in town understood the endeavor.

Homelessness, especially since the onset of the pandemic, had been an increasingly visible and seemingly intractable issue. On any given day there were more than 160,000 unhoused people in the state. Camps like the one Daniel had spent time at in San Rafael were cropping up all over, and especially across the Bay Area, where years of growing income inequality had already pushed the region into a houselessness epidemic. By the end of 2020, about 30 percent of all unhoused Americans lived in California. Among them were about seven thousand homeless households and more than ten thousand veterans like Daniel. In 2021, the state's governor, Gavin Newsom, cleared one hundred encampments a month, even showing up for photo ops of himself throwing out the belongings of tent city dwellers in Los Angeles and Berkeley. "Enough to fill 22 Olympic-size swimming pools," his office announced in a press release.

Since the onset of the pandemic, the state had invested hundreds of millions of dollars in new housing and social programs. But many Sausalito residents seemed to know intuitively that a solution to rising rates of homelessness wasn't coming anytime soon. After all, the city had never built any emergency shelters. And so, many came to support the anchor-outs. Though they often voiced their displeasure at Camp Cormorant, they also understood it. They donated money for portable toilets and a grill, as well as for fruit, spices, and canned and dried goods. Campers built a kitchen and stocked it with knives and bowls and pots. No one was denied food or water, and one resident, Sunny, made sure the whole setup stayed clean and sanitary. The residents built a small library, and artists painted the bay on driftwood, much as Bo had done not so long ago. They collected trash, kept pathways clean, and followed distancing guidelines from the Centers for Disease Control and Prevention (CDC), erecting tents at least six feet apart. Peter began to give sermons there, describing Camp Cormorant as an extension of the Pirate Church. He lived on $1,000 a month and estimated he spent one-fifth of that buying food for his congregation. An anchor-out known for nervously declaring himself to be Jesus Christ at city council meetings began showing up with an acoustic guitar. Jeff would stroll around with Daniel from time to time, singing "This Little Light of Mine."

22

BY EARLY FEBRUARY, THE CAMP HAD DRAWN THE ATTENTION OF THE mayor, who convened an emergency city council meeting.

"Mayor," a council member said before the roll call, "I was just wondering if we could discuss the nature of the special meeting, and why it is today." The camp comprised only a dozen tents. No major incident had been reported, and some on the council who had recently visited the camp found it clean and orderly.

"We are having it today because we need to take action on this matter," said the mayor.

The council member began to speak, but the mayor interrupted, saying, "I don't think at this point it is appropriate to go into why we are having the meeting."

"I just wanted to understand why we are doing this."

"Call the roll!" the mayor said, annoyed with the line of questioning.

The Sausalito police chief laid out the situation in Dunphy Park. Camp Cormorant had popped up in one of the most visible parts of town, along Bridgeway, near the yacht club. "We are concerned for the safety of the occupants," he said. "There is a lack of access to restrooms, showers, and other sanitary services, and those things present health, welfare, and safety risks to the people living in the encampment and to the environment."

Without easy access to running water and restrooms, the logic went, the anchor-outs were inevitably going outside to relieve themselves. The better alternative, as the chief, the mayor, and what already appeared to be a majority of the city council saw it, was to move the encampment a half-mile up the coast to Marinship Park, a small patch of grass and dirt in between the city's only public restroom, the tennis courts, and the Army Corps of Engineers yard. However, under this new proposal, known as Resolution 6009, the Marinship campers would be required to break down their tents a half-hour after dawn and allowed to set them up again no earlier than a half-hour before sunset.

The anchor-outs and the representation they had obtained from the California Homeless Union opposed the resolution. If the Marinship Park camp, as proposed by Resolution 6009, had to be torn down each day, there would be no way for the anchor-outs to form a community, to prepare food and solve problems together. And it was estimated that as many as half of the full-time campers were elderly or disabled. How, their advocates wondered, would they pick up their tents and belongings and carry them around all day? The city argued that the temporary nature of the camp would not be a problem, as the council was well on its way to what it called a "long-term solution" through which permanent housing on land would be found for everyone.

"We have a good record of demonstrating our commitment to finding alternatives for people who are living on Sausalito's waters," the chief said at the meeting. "Since 2017, our record is that we have reduced the number of vessels from ninety to nine."

Some of those ninety were now living at Camp Cormorant.

The council was not without its own concerns about the Marinship plan. The city manager took the microphone to tease out some possible legal challenges. "So you have all heard of the *Martin v. Boise* decision case by now? It's a Ninth Circuit Court of Appeals decision—federal court—that came out in 2018. The court ultimately held that the Eighth Amendment of the US Constitution prohibits cities from criminalizing indigent people without homes for sleeping outdoors on public property."

The decision stemmed from a case in which, between 2007 and 2009, six unhoused people in Boise were cited for violating a "camping ordinance," which made it a misdemeanor to use "any of the streets, sidewalks, parks or public places as a camping place at any time." The US Supreme Court refused to hear the City of Boise's appeal, and so, the city manager noted, the ruling was final. She pointed out that the Ninth Circuit contained the largest unhoused population in the United States. "It also includes California, obviously, and is binding on jurisdictions in California." She continued: "It's important to understand what *Boise* says and what it doesn't. The clear holding of *Boise* is that the protections apply only to persons who have no option of sleeping indoors and that cities still have the ability to regulate the location, essentially the time, place, and manner of sleeping outdoors as well as other reasonable regulations."

The city's lawyers assessed Resolution 6009 as being within the boundaries set by the Ninth Circuit. The circuit judge had found that the Eighth Amendment barred a city from punishing someone simply "for lacking the means to live out the 'universal and unavoidable consequences of being human.'" The city council had been on record for years assuring constituents that it had no plans to build emergency shelters in Sausalito, so in their absence, the city council would have to let people sleep somewhere. But, the city reasoned, as long as Marinship Park provided sufficient room, there was no clear reason why the unhoused couldn't be mandated to stay there. Nor was there any clear ruling on whether a city had to allow camping during the daylight hours. This question had arisen elsewhere: in Sacramento, for example, unhoused people were allowed to camp at night on the grounds of City Hall, but not during the day.

"I think we will move on to public comment," said the mayor, opening the conversation to the more than 150 residents in attendance.

"I would request that people who make public comments—of course we like passionate discussion here in Sausalito—but if you could please, um, work to make your comments respectful and with empathy and treat each other with kindness, I think we would all appreciate that."

Robbie was first in line.

"Okay, thank you," he said. "What I just want to really drive through is a recent study out of UC Berkeley showed that Sausalito was one of the most socially inequitable cities in the entire state, that the segregation of Sausalito, going back to the segregation of Marin City, going back to your council's decision to evict people living anchored out in Sausalito, all these are part of a pattern of incredible systemic disregard for human dignity, for people's voices to be heard, a desire to hoard and to create an artificial bubble while people are suffering, while people are just trying to get by. I heard from somebody who did a public records act request that the chief called our community a disorderly mess. Sunny's kitchen! *You saw the kitchen,*" he said, referring to a council member who had visited recently. "The *pride* of the kitchen down here! And he just, he doesn't care. There is no regard. There *is* a way forward. But Sausalito needs to contend with its racist, classist history. With that, I'm gonna hand it off."

"Hello, Mayor," said Jeff.

"Yeah . . . hello."

"Ahoy. This land has never been used as long as I've been here in Sausalito, twenty years, except for once, the police station was here. So rather ironic there is another policeman reclaiming this area— not for anything, but for an *absence* of something."

"Thank you."

"It was very interesting to me that the chief was so concerned about the environment," said the next speaker. "And I say that because it seems that our concerns about the environment stem mainly from when it is poor people who seem to be offending the environment. I'd like to point out that the anchor-outs and the unhoused community have a very very small carbon footprint." She was no doubt aware that in 2018 a San Francisco Bay Regional Water Quality Control Board official stated that an anchor-out's discharge into the bay was so insignificant as to be "very difficult to detect." The speaker continued: "I've never heard the chief complain about wealthy white property owners who have large homes in the hills of Sausalito and have additional properties in Hawaii, and fly business class or first class to Hawaii, to these second homes. So these white property owners are essentially hoarding property. They think it makes them great. But the rest of us have some other ideas about that. But in the process they are doing incredible destruction to the environment. We can't afford to have people living at that level anymore. Meanwhile, we have a pandemic, and we can't provide basic things because one of the things that made a lot of these people wealthy is the mass privatization of things like our public health infrastructure, and the financialization of housing. We are on the cusp of yet another foreclosure crisis because of the pandemic. It's staggering to me. So I ask that we take a more compassionate"—the speaking timer went off—"look at—"

"Your three minutes have elapsed," said the mayor.

On this occasion, many in town who had been notably silent on issues about the anchor-outs echoed these concerns, at least in part. For more than an hour, one after another, they raised questions for the city council:

"I don't see why we would move them. Is it just 'out of sight, out of mind'?"

"We are in the middle of a worldwide pandemic. The answer can't just be—I just don't get it."

"Why is the public spending their time on this item?"

"What the hell would we do if we had to break camp every day?"

"I see the tent encampment from my window. I'm not happy with it, but I fully understand why it is there."

"They are people that are down and out. It could be anybody, you lose your job."

"It's been way too long of a rift between the anchor-outs, the homeless, and it just is getting to be too wide of a gap."

"I've been to the encampment. It's nothing but communal, supportive, and peaceful."

"It sounds like this is a remedy of making them less visible and tending to what I imagine is pressure from our neighbors on our city government to not have poverty be visible on Bridgeway."

"The emergency isn't that we have an encampment now. The emergency started long before the COVID pandemic. Surrounding cities have had encampments for years. We are just joining them. An unhoused community is here to stay in Sausalito for the time being. And frankly, the proposed intervention sounds more like an effort to move these individuals out of sight or to harass them into leaving Sausalito altogether. We shouldn't do that. Our beloved houseboat community, once disdained by landed interest, started out in a very similar way."

In contrast, a resident supporting the passage of the resolution assured the council that in fact many who lived on the hill supported an effort to dismantle Camp Cormorant but were scared that speaking up would invite the wrath of the vocal minority they had just heard. "If you look at all the businesses that are in between Dunphy Park and the 7-Eleven—the massage yoga place and the caviar place!—these places are suffering. I *totally* feel compassion for these people, but this is not the right place."

"Okay," said the mayor. "At this point, I'm gonna close public comment and start the discussion up here with the council."

"I would love to follow up," said a member of the council. "I think that we have not explored every possible opportunity."

A new member, dressed in a suit and tie, disagreed: "We are faced with choosing the least bad option," he said. "It is not a solution for homelessness. It is not perfect. It is not joyful. It *is* compassionate."

"This issue is the requirement to decamp every day," another member said. "The impact of the pandemic, overlaid with the other really troubling issues of living with homelessness and experiencing homelessness, have convinced me that it may be better—at least during the pandemic—to not impose that requirement."

"We are all trying to do the right thing, right?" said the mayor, directing her attention to her dissenting colleagues. "Taking no action I don't think is really an option."

"I am hesitant to rush to an immediate solution right now."

"Respectfully, the council member knows as well as I do none of these answers are going to change," the mayor replied. "Delaying it is not going to help. That's my conclusion."

The member in the suit agreed. "We need to take action," he said. "The choice about breaking down the encampment—having to strike camp every day—is so that this location is *not* an encampment. It's not a permanent, it's not a semipermanent system of dwellings that deprives that area from the rest of the community. *Obviously*, it would be more comfortable for those who have to camp to have a place to be all day. It is *of course* a better way to live. I'm not proposing this as an attractive alternative way to live. It would be easy to fall down the rabbit hole of looking for a perfect solution."

"Honestly, I think we are at our decision point. We have three members who have indicated they are willing to vote for the resolutions as they are before us," said the mayor. "We have a motion, we have a second, please call the roll."

The council voted:

"Yes."

"No."

"Yes."

"I feel like we could have done better—but I will vote yes."

"Yes."

"Very good," said the mayor, adjourning the meeting.

A NOTICE TO VACATE WAS POSTED at Camp Cormorant four days later. The encampment, it read, was a hazard that posed "serious health, welfare, and safety risks to the persons living in the encampment and to the environment that adversely affect residential and commercial uses."

23

UPON SEEING THE NOTICE, THE ANCHOR-OUTS FILED SUIT AGAINST THE city.

In it, the camp members, who by mid-February numbered about twenty, argued that moving them to Marinship Park was wrong for several reasons: first and foremost, the CDC guidelines had advised municipalities without homeless shelters not to destroy camps during the pandemic. "Clearing encampments can cause people to disperse throughout the community," which "increases the potential for disease spread," the agency wrote. The unhoused of Sausalito had built a clean, socially distanced, and compliant dwelling. Why force them to relocate and then disperse every morning, putting the entire city at increased risk? And second, the new proposed site in Marinship Park was situated next to the Army Corps of Engineers boatyard, from which emanated "clouds of lead-based paint dust and fiberglass resulting from the daily boat crushing operations immediately adjacent to the park." Many of the boats being crushed were the very homes that they had been evicted from.

The court agreed, stating that the move would expose all parties to increased viral risk and put undue physical burdens on the unhoused and disabled, and that there was "practically no evidence of harm" in letting them stay. To the city's argument that the camp didn't have adequate facilities, the court pointed out that the anchor-outs had on their own procured a handwashing station and portable toilets. Moreover, the city had failed to show that there was any evidence of sewage spill. The court further pointed out that the city's claim that the nearby bathrooms were not accessible was based on the fact that the city itself had locked them, "which would appear to be a matter entirely within Defendant's control." As for showers, there were none simply because the city chose not to put them nearby. "The court does not find convincing Defendant's contention that the mobile showers cannot be placed and operated in proximity to Dunphy Park," wrote the judge, adding: "Although Defendants purport to be concerned about the health and safety of Dunphy Park campers, they have presented no evidence that city officials or employees have visited the camp and taken steps to ensure that, e.g., the CDC guidance on such encampments is being observed."

AND SO, AS SPRING PASSED, THE camp continued to grow. A small school tent was built, with a chalkboard used to teach the alphabet and the chemical makeup of cannabis. In a nearby library tent, there were maybe a few hundred books. Outside, Jeff planted a garden of sunflower sprouts to mitigate the heavy metals from the toxic soil the city stored under a tarp from the days of building Liberty ships. A bike-fixing station offered free transport to anyone who needed it. And Sunny's kitchen kept cooking up meals, using food and dry goods donated by locals.

The RBRA, meanwhile, pressed on with its enforcement of the Transition Plan. Many of the younger residents who could leave the anchorage had done so by that point. According to one anchor-out estimate, the average age on the water was about sixty-eight. As enforcement increased, the anchorage continued to shrink, disappearing into the boatyard of the Army Corps of Engineers. Backhoes ripped apart wood and fiberglass hulls, sending homes, sometimes passed down for decades, into the air. Front loaders scooped up trash, along with hand-me-downs, photo albums, artwork, and journals accumulated in the lifetimes of those who had left home, by choice or otherwise, and made their way on the water.

Sunny's boat was taken while she was on land at the camp, organizing the kitchen and planning a meal. Then Diane, Larry's wife, passed away at age seventy-five, still making art on the vessel where Larry and later Innate had lived, and where she resided with Handsome Harry and the rest of the cats. Upon her death, the harbormaster attempted to seize the boat, but Robbie and a group of anchor-outs jumped on board.

The harbormaster argued that the boat was polluting the bay.

A week later, hundreds of thousands of gallons of Marin County sewage leaked into the estuary when old line joints were ruptured by tree roots. The harbormaster moved on.

The potential for loss, even for a violent end, often led to one. The cautionary tales floated like flotsam around the camp. There was the man whose brother had his boat taken by the RBRA and crushed. Looking to avoid this fate, the man attempted to side-tie his two boats together, making them more difficult to seize. At some point in the operation, he slipped between the vessels and drowned. Afterward, both boats were crushed.

By May, the camp housed forty people. For all the sadness and loss, the anchor-outs had maintained their community, held it together. They shared meals and stories and hours of prayer. Survival, in some sense, still felt possible.

24

"WHAT THE HELL?" A BYSTANDER SHOUTED OVER THE SOUND OF A CHAIN-saw ripping through the cabin of Rose's old boat, the *Projectile*, now owned by an anchor-out named Michael.

It was mid-April, and the Marin County sheriff's Special Response Team (SRT), the equivalent of a SWAT team, was on the dock of the yacht club, trying to cut their way inside, where an anchor-out named Paul was holed up with his dog Runt.

By this point everyone had heard Paul's story. He had been living with Runt on his boat, the *Warlock*, when one day, while he was getting groceries on land, the harbormaster seized and began to tow it to the Army Corps of Engineers boatyard. There it likely would be classified as marine debris and destroyed. Accounts of the initial events differed, but according to Paul, he saw it happening from afar, boarded his skiff, and headed for the *Warlock* to tell the harbormaster it was his primary vessel, his home. Without it, he would be homeless, he said, and would have to join the very camp population the city was trying so hard to reduce. As Paul rowed out to the boat, he claimed, he fired a flare gun for help. The harbormaster claimed, however, that the flare was fired at him, only missing his boat by accident. And after he seized the *Warlock* and impounded it—placing on it a notice announcing that it, and everything inside, would be crushed in ten days—an arrest warrant was issued for Paul. In the meantime, Paul, now homeless, began staying with Michael on the *Projectile*. Police contacted him, asking him to surrender, but according to news reports published in the *Pacific Sun*, he instead "rambled, said he had a bulletproof vest and refused to give up." Paul believed himself to be a high-ranking officer in the military and a steamship magnate; he battened down the hatches and secured his position with Runt.

As the anchor-outs onshore looked on, deputies fired flashbangs and beanbag rounds and tear gas into the vessel. His reason for being inside, according to Michael, was that "he was afraid of going to jail and not being able to take care of his dog."

"I don't want to watch this, I'm going to have bad dreams later," said an anchor-out onshore over the screeching of the chainsaw slicing through plywood.

Once the hole was made in the cabin wall, the SRT pulled Paul from the boat and laid him out on the dock.

"They are trying to poke him with an oar or something."

"Is he alive?"

"I think so?"

As the officers arrested Paul, smoke began to billow from the vessel.

"Holy fuck!" one of the bystanders shouted to the officers.

"Jesus fucking Christ. There is twenty of you fuckers and nobody thought to get a fire extinguisher?"

"Oh, the fire guy is coming!"

"Oh yeah, there it is, a fireboat," someone said, referring to the Southern Marin Fire Department vessel sailing up to the scene.

"Hurry up!"

"Fucking twenty flashbangs and they didn't see that might happen?"

"Where is the dog?"

"The dog? I don't know."

"The dog might be in there!"

"The boat is on fire. It's going up in flames!"

"What the hell!?"

"You can see the flames coming out of the hatch."

"It's on fire!" they shouted at the officers, who were watching along with the fireboat.

"Guys, where is his dog?!"

The fireboat continued to stand by.

"Why aren't they putting it out?"

"They want it to be destroyed."

"Put the fucking fire out!"

"Look at it. It's fucking burning. They haven't thrown any water on it."

For some reason, almost twenty minutes passed before the firefighters attempted to extinguish the flames. Once they finally did, they boarded the vessel. Runt's body was found inside.

A FEW MONTHS AFTER THE FIRE, I met up with Jim in San Francisco.

We walked down the Embarcadero and ate pizza. He was still living up in Napa River, where he was awaiting parts for the *Tola Levine*. The homeless encampment in Sausalito was growing, he said, but he doubted there was any future for them or the anchorage. In the long run, the forces were just too great.

As we sat outside, eating in the cool bay breeze, I thought about the Embarcadero. It was where, more than a century ago, boats abandoned by prospectors from around the world were dragged up onto shore and converted into hotels, casinos, and bars. Eventually, after developers filled in the area and paved it, it became some of the most valuable commercial real estate in the city.

I asked Jim about the *Projectile*.

"Yeah," he said. "The fire department, two police forces, harbormaster, Coast Guard, all came for a guy who had PTSD," he said. "Pretty ridiculous to use a chainsaw."

What did he make of it?

Jim shook his head. Though Paul's case was later dismissed, the message was clear: it would never stop until both the anchorage and the encampment were gone. "They are just so bold in their war."

IN LATE JUNE, THE RESIDENTS OF Camp Cormorant woke up to a sign of the end that by this point they all knew was coming:

NOTICE TO VACATE
UNAUTHORIZED ENCAMPMENT

Pursuant to its authority under Sausalito Municipal Code
Section 13.28.010, the city has mandated the closure of
all city-owned and city-controlled property to overnight
camping, except the designated and signposted area within
Marinship Park (at Testa Street at Marinship Way) as a
transitional overnight camping location for individuals
who have no other option of sleeping indoors.

The public works department will clear and close this
site at approximately 10:00 AM on June 29, 2021.

IN LATE MAY, THE CDC HAD dropped its recommendation that municipalities desist from dismantling homeless encampments. The judge responded by lifting the injunction against Sausalito. They were now allowed to forcibly relocate the camp, he said.

Many of the members of Camp Cormorant refused to move. Their camp was clean, they had obtained bathrooms, and the space was nice. The grassy coastal park had long been their community space. They looked after each other, and residents of the hill volunteered time and resources to help them out. For all its hardships, it was a beautiful place. Marinship Park, on the other hand, was a fenced-in muddy lot, stuck between a boat-crushing yard and the cinderblock walls of a public restroom.

June 29 became known as Destruction Day, and to prepare for it, they put up signs across the camp: LET US BE FREE 2 PROSPER, LOVE WILL WIN, OPEN YOUR HEART. Those who prayed, prayed, and those who sang, sang. One artist set out a painting they'd done of the anchorage, with the orange sun setting on the few boats still remaining on the water.

25

IN THE EARLY HOURS OF THE MORNING ON JUNE 29, POLICE BEGAN TRICK-
ling into the camp to warn the anchor-outs to move their belongings.

Daniel stood at the entrance, holding an American flag and
wearing pajamas and a tall, pointed cap that, with his long white
hair and beard, made him look like a garden gnome. Robbie stood
next to him in a Homeless Union shirt, waving the rainbow Camp
Cormorant flag.

Daniel began to shout. "I am proud to hold this flag, I am thankful for the Constitution of the United States. That gives me the formal
authority to stand here and praise God and give thanks that this is a
totally *public* hearing."

Anchor-outs gathered around him.

"This is *family* business," he said to the police. "No government
is involved. No corporation is involved. Everyone with a belly button
is invited. There is only one Family of God. And we are here."

He raised the flag higher.

Nearby, an anchor-out with a bushy beard was sitting on a concrete Jersey barrier on which a sign was resting that said CORRUPTION.
He was a few feet from one of the portable toilets that the city had
repeatedly claimed the anchor-outs did not have access to, or were not
using.

Detritus from those who had cleared out was blowing across the
grass.

A police officer with a mask approached from the opposite side.
"They are not going to be here until ten," the cop said, referring to

the front loader that would rip the camp apart. "That's when this whole thing is supposed to start."

The anchor-out looked at him in disbelief. He had long hair and wore clothes too heavy for the season.

"You got time," he said, in an encouraging and friendly way. "A little bit. Not days. But manpower, whatever you need." He was there, he assured the anchor-out, to help.

"Yeah," the anchor-out said. "I just think three days was just too short."

"Yeah . . . well . . ."

"It's cruel. After six months of allowing people to live somewhere, and then giving them a seventy-two-hour notice to leave."

"It's transitional."

"Do you think that's right? I mean, just stop and think about it."

"It's—"

"No! Think about it. Put yourself in that position."

The officer leaned back on his heels. Another anchor-out, a large man maybe in his fifties who had been listening to the exchange, joined the conversation. "It was all right then, but isn't it all right now? What the fuck is up with that?"

"Well," the cop said through his mask, "COVID has ended. And the judge decided that it's okay now."

The man said he had been up in Sebastopol helping his mom, but came back down for Destruction Day. He simply wanted to care for his elderly parents, but the city wouldn't let him: for reasons that he still couldn't grasp, he had to return to Sausalito just to move his dwelling a few minutes' walk away. For what?

The cop shrugged. "We're doing the best we can. Does anyone need help with stuff?"

The bearded anchor-out on the barrier scoffed. "I heard you were helping Caroline," he said, referring to another Camp Cormorant resident. "She said you ripped up her tent."

"I'll get her a new tent," the cop replied. "It was an accident if

I did. But I'll get her a new tent. No problem. It wasn't intentional, and I didn't even know I did it. So . . . I was just trying to get the bed out of that opening. It's tiny. But yeah . . . sorry. We help out. I'm not perfect."

"But why would someone want help from someone who would make them leave?"

"But I'm not the—I'm the guy, I'm the face I guess—but I'm not the one making the choices, man."

"You're the one here."

"I know, that's what I'm telling you. I'm the messenger. I'm not the guy that's making the message."

Just then, a woman emerged from behind the portable toilet, as a few more anchor-outs gathered around. "You are not a messenger!" she shouted at the cop. "You make a choice! Every morning. With what you are going to do with your time and your heart!"

"Right."

"And this is what you are choosing to do."

"Yesterday I spent eight hours helping—"

"This is what you are choosing to do! Right now. You have a human choice." She approached the barrier and started pointing at him. "Stop what you are doing. You can walk away and use your heart."

Daniel walked up behind her with the American flag.

She continued, pointing her finger at the officer: "But that's not what you are choosing. Don't act like you don't have a choice! Shame on you!"

A few of the anchor-outs grew annoyed with the shouting woman. "You are misrepresenting us," one said.

"Go have another drink," said another.

The woman walked away.

Daniel approached the officer, still holding the flag, and said: "The choice you have is right now."

"I'm just trying to help you guys. I get it," the cop replied.

A woman in the crowd called out to him: "How can you help us keep the anchorage?"

AS TEN O'CLOCK APPROACHED, A LARGE yellow front loader rumbled through the parking lot, toward the entrance of the camp. Police crowded around it, attempting to make way for the machine.

Robbie and Daniel walked down to meet it. Several officers tried to stop them.

"Don't touch me! Don't touch me!" Daniel began to shout, angry in a way he didn't usually show.

Robbie put his hands out and stepped between the police and Daniel. One of the officers grabbed the Camp Cormorant flag and dropped it to the ground. Another took Robbie's wrist.

The group of anchor-outs grew. They demanded to know why Robbie was being detained. Jeff appeared among them, dressed all in red, holding the Hebrew Bible and the sort of plastic megaphone they give away at sporting events, and exclaimed: "The Lord spoke to Moses!—this is 26:52—Among these the land shall be divided for inheritance, according to the number of the names. To a large tribe he shall give a large inheritance, and to a small tribe he shall give a small inheritance. Every tribe shall be given inheritance in proportion to its list. The land shall be divided by lot. It's called Jubilee! Everybody gets a place to live!"

As Jeff read, Daniel approached the officers once more. "You can just ignore the law. And think because you have a badge and gun you can do it. You are under orders like a good Nazi. 'Oh, I can't help it, it is my job!'"

Jeff held up the Hebrew Bible again and started singing. "*We shall not, we shall not be moved . . .*"

The front loader shook to life and crawled up toward the tents.

"Ohhh no! What's this going on?" said Daniel, standing in front of it.

In the distance, a drum was beating.

"Every one of you is testing me!" Daniel said. "You are *all* in trouble now. You have organized and planned this treasonous activity."

He pointed at the giant front loader, whose bumper had a sign warning people not to get run over.

"Whoever you are defending, it is not God, and it is not me, and it is not the people of the United States. Or the people of the world."

Chains dragged away barriers as police and city workers assembled a chain-link fence around the site. Soon, all that was left would be crushed by bulldozers, scooped up by backhoes, and hauled away in dumpsters.

"You're committing a massive crime under the color of law and you don't even know it!" Daniel continued as the end began. "You don't know the penalties for what you are doing. I am warning you, in Jesus's name." He pointed up to the sky. "There is a God right now. Here!" He made the sign of the cross. "You don't believe it? You are gonna believe it."

26

AFTER DESTRUCTION DAY, FORTY OR SO ANCHOR-OUTS WERE RELOCATED up the shore, in Marinship Park. There they were tightly packed together just across the fence from the Army Corps of Engineers yard, where many of their boats had been crushed.

On a drizzly afternoon in August of 2021, I found Robbie marching through the new camp. Tents were organized on a grid, into blocks of six or eight. Lotus was wandering along the muddy pathways, picking up trash.

What grass there may have once been was now trampled over. There were both simple tents and large plywood structures that looked like cabins from the boats they used to live on. American and rainbow Pride flags were draped over dwellings. Near the entrance was a large open-air tent protecting a gas stove, donated by someone in town. They'd rebuilt Sunny's kitchen: there was shelving with dried goods, beans, and rice. There were pots, pans, knives, and cutting boards. A rail-thin woman was talking fast and angrily, about what I couldn't hear. Jeff and a few other anchor-outs were listening from a nearby picnic table.

It was chilly, and getting colder, when an anchor-out named Tim approached me and Robbie in distress.

There was a woman in the camp screaming, he told Robbie, and no one could figure out how to calm her down.

Robbie ran off to help, but Tim stayed behind with me.

"I want to show you something," he said.

His coat looked too heavy for his shoulders as he led me through a row of tents, over to the fence on the eastern side of the encampment. He peered through it at the Army Corps of Engineers facility, at a large dumpster filled with the remnants of a crushed vessel. We slipped through a hole in the fence and walked over to the yard.

The boat, he said, belonged to a friend of his. The Corps' giant red crane had dragged it out of the water, lifted it into the air, and dropped it onto the concrete ramp, sending a plume of fiberglass dust into the air. She had no choice but to watch her home be destroyed, Tim explained, as the city had mandated that those evicted from their boats live in the camp. He told me that many anchor-outs believed that the Army Corps of Engineers made a point of dragging the vessels along the ground as they were crushed, so that their owners would hear the noise. Tim said that when the woman began to scream in panic, someone in the small audience that had gathered to enjoy the demolition began throwing rocks at her.

I looked Tim over. Recounting the story made him nervous.

He didn't know what to make of it, he said. Of any of it. Last night, a man no one had ever seen before showed up in the camp and, by the account of some who were there, assaulted a woman. Tim began to shake as he spoke. He said he had called the police, but no one, as far as he knew, came to investigate. "I'd never called police before in my life—now I see why people don't."

Tim's phone rang, and he told me he'd be right back.

I turned toward the camp.

A couple was arguing in their tent. On the anchorage, each person had lived in relative solitude, spread out over a mile of water. They sailed to one another's boats often, to exchange stories and vegetables, play music, help with repairs, and go fishing. But they had their own homes, decorated with family photos, letters from children and parents, mattresses and blankets. All of that was gone.

"I'm afraid for my life," I overheard Tim say on the phone.

When he returned, he slipped his phone in his pocket and wiped his hands on his dirty jeans.

I asked him if everything was okay.

He didn't answer.

Back at the picnic table, I sat down with Jeff, Daniel, a man named Chappy, and a few anchor-outs I'd never seen before.

Robbie returned from trying to help the woman who had been panicking in her tent. He shook his head. "It's a genocide," he said, looking over the encampment, as worn-down anchor-outs crawled from the entrances of their vinyl shelters to trudge through the last hours of daylight and find what they could afford to eat at the nearby 7-Eleven. "That's what it is."

Everyone at the table began to discuss the use of the word "genocide."

A man sat down at the table with a bowl of something from the kitchen. "The extermination of a culture of people," he said, spooning the food into his mouth. "*That* is genocide."

Strange, said another anchor-out, who had seemed lost in thought. He bent around to survey the encampment, then noted that, their numbers having been cut in half in the space of two years, the anchor-outs had endured "something akin to the erasure of a culture."

An anchor-out reached over to hand some weed to Jeff, who was in a black Stetson hat, his curly salt-and-pepper hair and beard flowing out of it.

"I can't ignite on the Sabbath," he said.

The guy moved to take back his bowl.

Jeff waved him off and handed him the lighter. "*I* just can't *ignite* on the Sabbath," he said.

The guy lit the bowl for Jeff. He took a deep breath and let loose a white cloud across the table.

Chappy handed Jeff and me a pair of beers.

I took a sip, but it was cold and I began to shiver.

A man standing next to me stepped into a nearby plywood dwelling, then reemerged a moment later with a large white blanket.

He draped it over my shoulders and told me to be careful, because there was wet paint on one side.

I asked him what he was painting.

He said he was Native American, and he was redesigning the US flag with rainbow stars. "The country of the world," he said.

I kept shivering. Beneath the blanket I still couldn't get warm on the wet muddy ground.

Daniel took off a puffy 49ers coat he was wearing and gave it to me. I put it on, and he patted my shoulder and smiled, as if admiring a good patch job.

JEFF AND I WENT TO SMITTY'S to warm up.

I hadn't been inside the bar since the coronavirus pandemic started, now almost two years ago. The place was packed. The Giants were playing the Rockies on a television in the corner. The entire bar hung on the tie game.

I wondered to Jeff whether a bartender I had known years ago still worked there.

"Why?" he asked.

She had a book that Bo wrote in the seventies, called *Afrobozodiac*.

Jeff was intrigued.

She emailed me some pages, I said. They contained illustrations of Bo in what appeared to be swimwear, with lines connecting the elbows to the head and groin, along which he had written text such as: "Sex organs → water → ← Scorpio ← Neck-Face-Earth."

I didn't know what to make of it.

Jeff laughed. The anchorage had changed so much, he said. The community had been decimated. He was worried about how it all looked from the outside. The violence and unhappiness were not inherent to life on the estuary. But an incredible bureaucratic force had taken everyone from their boats. Pillars of the anchorage had died and disappeared. The ever-present stress—from the constant crushing of vessels, from the knowledge that everything would come to end— had taken its toll. Anchor-outs had sometimes decades-long ties to Marin County. There was nowhere else for them to go. Most of those living in the Marinship encampment were not unhoused because of some mental illness. Now, however, some were losing themselves.

Still, Jeff said, he understood the limits to this misery. The Messiah would come, and all would be made right. The wicked would be punished, and the boats would rise with the tides.

As we finished our beers, the bar erupted in cheers. The Giants had won.

"Go Giants!" some men at the bar shouted as we headed back to the camp.

LOTUS WAS AT THE TABLE NOW, and Dream had pulled up next to her in his wheelchair. A man named Tom was reading them a poem he had written.

When he finished, he asked me what I thought.

Very Irish, I told him.

Lotus laughed and nodded her head.

I asked him what the poem was about.

Tom explained that, long ago, when he was young, he was a dancer in New York City. But nothing ever came of his auditions; in the end, it just didn't happen for him. He was sad about it at the time, but like all things, he learned to see it differently with age.

I looked over to the kitchen area, where a young woman was cooking.

I asked Dream how he was holding up during the pandemic.

"I'm not hard up," he said. "I'm just in a wheelchair."

Had he avoided the coronavirus?

"The whole thing is a farce," he said, adding that he never got sick because he had a good immune system.

I disagreed.

Lotus shook her head at me. I was of course free to see things differently, she explained, but first I should consider what he was saying. They were both much older than me. I might be too young to understand. But if I just aligned my chakras, she said through a coughing bout, I would survive coronavirus.

AS WE TALKED INTO THE NIGHT, the sound of flesh pounding metal echoed from the men's bathroom. A woman inside was screaming.

I was alarmed at first, but one of the guys at the table explained that this was a nightly ritual. Each day, after the sun set, the woman got out of her tent and walked into the men's room to scream and smash her fists into the walls and toss around anything that wasn't screwed down.

When she emerged from the bathroom, the young woman in the kitchen began to argue with her. "You're a fucking bitch!" she said.

The woman from the bathroom shouted back something about a man who murdered two people.

Tim walked up, and she told him she was afraid of the murderer. She begged him to let her have a knife from the kitchen, but he refused. Getting angrier, the woman turned to me and started yelling.

I looked to the group at the table and asked if I had done something wrong.

"No," someone said. "It's just that you exist."

Eventually I lost track of the woman. I asked if it was safe for me to use the bathroom.

"Yeah, she is in her cage," he said.

Her cage?

He pointed over to her tent, which looked as if someone had built a little fence around it. "She built it for herself."

The night wound down, and eventually Lotus brought me a blanket and showed me to a dwelling they'd made in the corner, from plywood. I unfurled my sleeping bag and lay down to sleep as the shouting began once more.

THE NEXT MORNING I WOKE UP in the 49ers jacket, realizing I had forgotten to return it to Daniel. I walked over to his tent and knocked on the flap.

I apologized for keeping it overnight.

He stepped out and hugged me. "You are welcome here," he said.

I walked over to the kitchen area, where a woman was at the stove cooking eggs for everyone. She turned around. It was the same woman who, the previous night, had been screaming in the bathroom.

She smiled, wished me a good morning, and made me an egg.

27

THROUGHOUT THE WINTER OF 2021, ANCHOR-OUTS HAD EXPRESSED CON-
cerns over safety at the Marinship encampment. They were far more
vulnerable than they had been on the water. Strangers would enter
the camp and, according to anchor-outs, attack residents. The close
quarters and cold muddy nights had put everyone on edge. Fights
broke out more often. When they called the police, they alleged, no
one came. Or if they did, the police refused to investigate. Occasionally, the camp members said the officers themselves got violent.

The two sides met at a city council meeting to address the issue.

"Was there any sort of discussion with the chief about having
our police department handle this?" the vice mayor asked.

"I think that in the interest of creating a more reasonable environment for folks, having the police department there, um, probably
is not what they want to see," replied the city manager. "And it's
probably a lot more expensive."

A city council member nodded in agreement: "So, you have
mentioned that our costs on the encampment are now north of half
a million dollars. So, I just want to absorb that."

"When I talk about a half-million dollars I am talking about our
legal costs," said the manager. "I'm not sure as to the real number . . .
But I can say we have basically been footing this with city taxpayer
money."

"So, we are being asked tonight to allocate up to $185,000 for
security personnel?"

When the mayor moved on to public comment, Jeff jumped

in: "Half a million dollars is not being spent for services, Sausalito citizens. This is being spent for very high-priced lawyers to fight the homeless. That is where the money is being spent. There is zero money—zero—being spent for the homeless people of Sausalito. This is not only job production for consultants and for lawyers. This issue, these problems, this crisis if you want to call it that, is that money is being spent and it never comes to the people that can use it. In San Rafael, where there is a twenty-four-hour security guard, they are throwing food over the fence to feed the people. The process to feed the people is too burdensome. They do not allow visitors into the camp. There is not a chance in the world that that will fly in Sausalito. It is not going to happen that way. If somebody would like to come and talk with us, we can talk with you. But the idea that we are going to be providing money to high-priced lawyers, to consultants, to agencies, and to security guards because there are people without houses is completely corrupt."

"This," said Robbie, "has been a *massive* failure. The city promised that you were gonna be providing a safe place to live. That was part of the movement from there. And right now the city has failed . . . We call the police where there are crimes being committed . . . and the police come out and they don't do anything . . . What is needed is housing. Unless there is a way to lock your door. That's security right there. $185,000. Think about that. That's like what? $700 every month for every individual in this camp. You could be putting people in a room with that kind of money. Starting with vulnerable people who have been out here with broken hips, suffering from dementia, in wheelchairs. Nothing, nothing. Sausalito has not housed a single person. Nothing. There has been nothing. That is a tremendous failure of the city. And people need to be just shocked. We are gonna be coming up to . . . $800,000—not one person housed."

"Not one!" Jeff shouted.

The mayor did not exactly disagree: "Failure to house anyone from the Sausalito encampment in the last seven months is not acceptable. In the meantime, we need to institute some additional measures at our encampment, specifically security and the ability to connect people to services. Which is not being fulfilled by the nonprofit that is engaged by the county. So I would suggest that we adopt the resolution . . . authorizing the use of enhanced security."

A city council member asked for more clarity on the resolution: "I'm a little worried, because if it is specific, just all for security 24/7 for six months, I really want to be clear that half of it goes to services, or that it is for three months of security. Because we know the cost of security. And I think we really need a collaborative approach. I just want to really be clear that it's not all dedicated to 24/7 security. And if we are going to do it that way, then we would have security and have services and do it for a period of three months. So we would know that we have at least half and half."

"Yeah, so, I don't think you should get hung up on the six-month part," said the mayor, while agreeing to add language about "services" to the resolution. "So moved? Yes. Second? Okay, thank you. Madam Clerk, can you please take the roll?"

"Sorry, somewhere in the resolution can we say we will have a collaborative discussion with the residents about the security or the type of security services?"

"That's understood. Please let's just vote—"

"Okay, so—"

"For the love of God! Vote!"

The clerk tallied the vote.

"Motion passes."

28

INCREASINGLY, THE MEMBERS OF THE CAMP SEEMED AWARE THAT EYES were on them.

The extent of this concern was clear to me one night that fall at the Bridgeway 7-Eleven, which was known regionally for selling a scratcher worth three-quarters of a million dollars in 2016. There the anchor-outs disposed of their trash in the dumpster and bought hot dogs and taquitos when they had a few extra dollars. They bought beer and cigarettes there too, being unable to afford the prices at the wine shops farther down Bridgeway. Open twenty-four hours, the store had long attracted criticism from members of the community who were not pleased with the late-night activity.

One evening I ran into Tim in the parking lot. He was talking with a man in a tank top who was holding his dog's leash. I was staying at the camp that night and had come by to pick up some beer as a thank-you for the hospitality.

Do you guys need anything? I asked the two men.

Tim shook his head.

"Muscle Milk and a Sharpie," the man said.

Inside, I found the Muscle Milk, a protein powder that is no doubt useful if your meals are few and far between. But there was no Sharpie.

Outside, I told the man they didn't sell markers. As Tim rifled through his bag, I asked him what he thought the guy needed a Sharpie for. He shrugged. A moment later, Tim stopped short, pulled a Sharpie from his pocket, and handed it to the other man.

On the way back down to camp, the guy in the tank top noticed that the case of beer was getting the better of my arms.

"Do you want to trade?" he asked, offering me the dog leash.

Accepting, I marched at the dog's pace down the hill.

When we arrived at the camp, it was cold and completely dark. Leaning against a barricade at the entrance was a sign on which someone had scribbled with a marker in big black letters: STOP CRUSHING OUR BOATS.

We sat at the picnic table while the man in the tank top disappeared down one of the tent rows. I said hello to Jeff as the woman who howled at night in the bathroom commenced her screaming. No one seemed particularly concerned as she wandered into the parking lot.

After a few minutes, the man in the tank top returned and asked me if I could continue to look after his dog for a while. Agreeing, I left the commotion in the kitchen and brought the animal over to an open patch of muddy, worn-down grass. He was friendly and liked to play-bite, so I gave him my hand to chew on. A few minutes later, a group of anchor-outs I didn't recognize approached me, visibly upset. What did I think I was doing, allowing the dog to put my hand in his mouth?

He was just playing, I said.

Of course they knew that, they told me. But the Hill People, the police, the tourists, none of them knew that. It looked, from afar, like the dog was dangerous, like the anchor-outs were dangerous for keeping him around, for not disciplining him. They went on to explain: The situation in Sausalito had changed considerably. Rumors were circulating that the town wanted to bring in twenty-four-hour security. I had to understand, they told me, that for many anchor-outs, their boats had been or would soon be destroyed. As bad as the camp was, they had nowhere else to go. They couldn't afford for things to get any worse.

"Try to be more dominant," one said, disappointed, as they walked away.

I rejoined Jeff and a few other camp residents near the kitchen area. The screaming woman had disappeared into the darkness.

A few minutes later, a police officer approached our conversation. No one seemed surprised.

I asked Jeff what was going on.

He turned to me and sighed: "She called the cops on herself."

The familiar noise of metal clashing started up in the bathroom. Neither the cop nor the anchor-outs knew what to do. The screamer was bad for everyone's interests. They'd tried to diffuse it in the press. Peter had told a *Tam News* high school student reporter, "You see babblers and yellers and screamers. It's like primal scream therapy. There's a lot of threats and bluster and bluff, but it's like one big family, there's brothers and sisters fighting."

They passed the time with one another, making small talk about nothing, until the noise subsided and the woman emerged. The cop looked back at the group and sighed. "All right," he said as he walked away.

When, at last, the man returned for his dog, I went to bed.

THE NEXT MORNING I AWOKE TO a loud crunching sound.

Lotus came in a few minutes later. "Oh, I'm glad you are still here," she shouted over the clanging sounds. "I brought you some orange juice."

The noise, like nails on a chalkboard, was all-consuming. I asked her what it was.

It was somebody's boat, she said. The city was crushing it.

I could hear Daniel in a shouting match with someone outside, over a receipt.

How many boats, I thought, must have been crushed? How many times had the noise of collapsing hulls and shattering cabin windows rung out along the shoreline? When I first arrived in the anchorage in 2015, I heard estimates of more than two hundred boats on the water. Now perhaps twelve were left in Sausalito, and maybe a few dozen more farther out in RBRA waters. I brought it up to Lotus, but she didn't want to think about it.

"Rich and poor people suffer the same exact fear," she said, shaking her head. "The poor person says, 'I don't know where the next meal is coming from.' The rich person says, 'How do I protect what I have?'"

I took a sip of the orange juice and tried to hand it back to her.

She waved me off. "If you stay in one place long enough, everything will come to you," she said.

29

A FEW DAYS LATER, I PHONED INNATE, WHO WAS STILL LIVING IN THE ARI-
zona desert.

"Hey, brother," he said. "I got a Chevy Tahoe now—I'm *at home.*"

In the five years since Innate left the anchorage, he and Melissa
had built a self-sustaining farm, with a main house, a shed, and
a greenhouse. They had clean running water, a warm shower, and
friends in the neighborhood, none of which he had had since he was
arrested for growing weed all those decades ago in San Diego. He'd
changed, he said. And the world had changed too.

"I got a job," he told me on the phone, explaining that he'd been
hired by a company located twenty minutes from his property.

What are you doing? I asked.

"Take a wild guess."

Gardening?

"Very good! I'm what you call a bio spotter. My job is to nurture
plants."

I must have sounded confused.

"I grow pot," he laughed. "How cool is that? I don't do modding
on *Grand Theft Auto* anymore, but I get to grow."

Inspecting marijuana leaves for mildew was a welcome distraction, he told me. Melissa had left Arizona to see her family in Texas.
"We don't know what or how long or anything like that. It has been
an advantage, because it has brought us closer in different ways."

I asked him whether he thought she would ever return to the
desert.

"It has only been about a month that she has been in Texas. She's been through these experiences with her grandmother and her mother and her father. I'm being as understanding as I can, but I'm like, are we gonna get through this? But it's all about faith at this point. She collected up most of her items on this last Saturday . . ."

He trailed off; the phone went silent.

"There are all these strangenesses that if I want to look at it in the worst ways, then it's the worst. She has just done a change of address. She's gonna be there for an undetermined amount of time. Best, it is gonna be a few years."

I asked again about her coming back.

He waved off the question; it was no use looking at everything in such a negative way. He'd been bogged down his whole life in that habit and wasn't going to think that way anymore. To him, there had to be a better way of framing it, a "recalibration ability" to understanding the changes around him as something more than tragedy. "It's all there," he said. "It's what we want to stare at and what we want to talk about. I'm realizing I keep talking about the struggles without identifying those successes." He offered an example: "I lost teeth in the front—two of them," he said. "But the job that I have? I'm getting paid fifteen dollars an hour. For a guy like me, who lives off one hundred bucks a month, fifty bucks a month, that's a lot. So I can get my teeth fixed. I'll be a brand-new bionic me."

INNATE HAD FIRST ARRIVED AT THE anchorage decades ago, after his U-Haul was stolen from the Rainbow gas station, only to find that his new paradise was at times an inhospitable place. There were the harbormasters banging at his door, the friends cycling through court and jail, the storms and swells, the cracked hulls and frozen motors, the lost anchors, the stolen dinghies, the cold morning feet that no quilt could console. Having now lost Melissa to Texas, it would have been easy to slip back again into his anchorage state of mind, into what he called "The Big Fear—being scared of losing it all." But he refused.

Of course, time *had* validated the fear he'd felt in Sausalito. When he departed Richardson Bay in 2016, there were well over two hundred boats on the estuary, harboring more live-aboards than at any other time in at least the past century. Now, six years later, only a few dozen anchor-outs remained. And the RBRA had pledged to evict all of the holdouts by 2026. In Sausalito waters, the decline of the anchor-outs was even more pronounced. When Innate had lived on Larry's boat, just off Liberty Dock, he had about ninety neighbors within the city's jurisdiction. Today only seven were still afloat. Had he stayed on the water, in all likelihood he would have lost everything.

As to what happened to all those people, many of whom had no state-issued identification, no bank account, no registered address? No one really knows. But during the pandemic, as the anchorage was dismantled and the housing crisis worsened, the number of un-housed people living in cars and RVs in Sausalito increased from two to over seventy. The camps, at their peak, held around forty tents; it is estimated that some 150 campers passed through them. Among that group, an informal survey conducted by the *San Francisco Chronicle* identified at least five people who died shortly after leaving. I'd heard rumors of anchor-outs ending up in the San Rafael camp, or down in the Tenderloin in San Francisco. The idea of some of the anchor-outs getting to San Francisco always came across as wishful thinking, a hope that those who vanished had made it out there, somewhere across the bay.

"It'll bloom back up," Innate said of Richardson Bay. "Maybe this whole COVID aspect is the beauty in the beast. There was a great honest effort done that enabled our earth. Jets weren't flying. Factories weren't pumping out. Look at what happened to Italy. Their waters turned turquoise blue, and they saw dolphins swimming in them. We had a good thing happen here. We can kind of restart. It's a double-edged sword."

I asked: But what good had there been in all this for the anchor-outs?

"Have you seen *Free Guy*?"

I told him I hadn't.

"It's Ryan Reynolds. Do you know the actor? It is basically a story about a video game like *Grand Theft Auto* . . ."

For the rest of the call, he waited out the worst of Arizona's midday sun recounting the movie's plot. Ryan Reynolds is a nonplayable character in a massively multiplayer online role-playing game. That is to say, he is just an extra programmed to repeatedly perform a simple task again and again, to add some color to the world, some background for the living, human players. In the game, Reynolds is a bank teller working, on a loop, at a meaningless desk job as the main characters pass through his life on the way to their next adventure. Until one day he becomes aware of his circumstance. This new understanding sets him free. He falls in love with a woman who sings his favorite song, and he takes control of his source code. He travels around, teaching the other nonplayable characters what he has learned. At long last, he liberates them from the grind into which they have been programmed, and they go off to star in a game of their own.

"So?" Innate asks me, confirming that I'd understood the moral of the story before he had to head off to the marijuana farm. "Which way am I gonna see it?"

I wasn't sure what he meant.

"You experience—or you *bear witness*."

Of course, Innate hadn't witnessed what had happened to the anchorage. He hadn't seen how the residents of hundreds of boats had been evicted, driven away, and reduced to a few dozen people living in muddy tents. One could hardly imagine that they would call the experience liberating. None of them would be finding their desert paradise anytime soon.

30

MANY OF THE CAMPERS NO LONGER SHARED INNATE'S HOPE THAT THE anchorage, through means both legal and divine, would bloom again on the water.

Conditions in the encampment continued to deteriorate in the rainy final months of 2021. Lowly situated in a flood-prone area between the hill and the shore, Marinship Park was plagued with storm runoff. Its vulnerable position had been noted by the Homeless Union representing the anchor-outs a year earlier, when the city first proposed it as a relocation site for Camp Cormorant. But by the time the camp was relocated, Sausalito was in the midst of its dry summer months, when the hills of Northern California were yellow and the grass was crunchy.

Up until then, the park had been manageable enough for the anchor-outs, though soggy at times. And they'd proposed simple solutions, like pallets to use as platforms for their tents. The city had indicated some willingness to offer help. But when the National Weather Service began warning in October that an atmospheric river would soon drop more rain on the Bay Area than the region had seen in the previous three months combined, the city had yet to provide assistance and instead, the night before the storm broke, just dropped off sleeping bags.

On the evening of October 23, light showers began to fall over Marinship Park. Soon the winds, later clocked at 56 miles per hour, kicked up. Throughout Sausalito, almost a thousand homes went dark. More than 100 trees were ripped from the ground and strewn across roadways by cascading mud and rockslides, blocking responses to the more than 650 calls to the fire department made in the county that night. Debris clogged the drainage system, causing more than 80,000 gallons of sewage to overflow. Almost 200 homes flooded, and three buildings burst into flames.

The details of what occurred in the Marinship camp that night would emerge the following day, in accounts offered by anchor-outs at a city council meeting, where the mayor declared a state of emergency. "Equipment was destroyed—generators, power tools—it was adequately described as a disaster zone. The fencing collapsed, there was debris flying," said one resident. "By 4:00 a.m., people were screaming, there was chaos, the fences were collapsing, there was flying debris with nails, most of the people had been evacuated that time, trying to find any means of shelter other than at Marinship Park, it was completely flooding, the soil has a stench of contamination . . . At 4:00 a.m., we had someone who was screaming. I attempted to evacuate her multiple times as well as multiple people. She refused. By 5:30 a.m., my tent, the advocacy tent, was struck with flying debris and collapsed on me, and at that point I had no alternative but to evacuate. By 6:00 a.m., there was standing room only in the bathrooms, and the floor was coated with mud. It was horrific. It was absolutely horrific. I went back to try to clear the camp and was yelling, in particular who may still be here, Mr. Dream Weaver, and I went back to try to make sure that he was evacuated."

Meanwhile, for the last few dozen anchor-outs on the water, conditions were just as dire. Three live-aboard vessels were washed onto shore. Two more homes sank, and at least five skiffs, which were essential for getting to land, were lost. Asked later by a reporter about the sunken homes, the harbormaster said that they were "a safety and environmental problem." The newly unhoused residents, he added, needed to "make sure" that "this doesn't happen."

The camp would never truly recover. A local builder tried to erect a storage shed in which the anchor-outs could put any of their surviving personal items and family heirlooms during the next storm. But halfway through the construction, the city demanded that they obtain a permit. When they applied, the city never responded. Instead, two days later, Sausalito's building inspector posted a second notice informing the campers that unless they dismantled the structure, the city would demolish it.

A handful of the residents moved back to Dunphy Park. It wasn't the cold, muddy grass of Marinship Park that forced them out so much as the rancid liquid they claimed had started bubbling up from the ground. Robbie estimated that about a half-dozen anchor-outs developed skin and throat infections, as well as sores and abscesses in their mouths. For its part, the city did not acknowledge the contamination concerns. But to the anchor-outs, it was clear: the town's aging sewer system was pumping human waste from the residents on the hill into their encampment. The irony was not lost on anyone who'd been around a few years earlier and spent a long night or two in the hull of John's boat, alongside Keven, listening to the pair argue, seemingly in vain, that it was the city's runoff polluting the bay, not the anchor-outs. The BCDC and the RBRA, they maintained, should have been ticketing the residents on the hill for their inadequate sewer system and contaminated soil. Wasn't that the BCDC's job?

Members of the Marinship Park camp, through the Homeless Union, were able to commission a bacteriological exam from a nearby laboratory, which confirmed the elevated levels of fecal matter, which could cause hepatitis A and respiratory infections. The city said that it would conduct its own test. On the day it did, it also evicted the anchor-outs who had moved to Dunphy Park. They camped out on the lawn of City Hall instead.

By mid-November, the city had acknowledged the fecal contamination of the site. It announced that the new location for the encampment would be the nearby tennis courts, which one of the lawyers for the California Homeless Union described as "prison-like," and residents described as a "concentration camp," a "jail," and a "cage," all owing to the high fences surrounding the hard, cold courts that the dwindling group would be forced to sleep on. As the lawsuit played out in court and the harsh weather of the winter months of early 2022 pounded the encampment, allegations of arson and violence became commonplace. Anchor-outs and city officials would debate the veracity of these claims, but one was certainly accurate: in February, a camp resident in her sixties set her tent and her neighbor's tent on fire. The blaze spread to a nearby propane tank, which exploded, sending a thirty-foot column of blue flame over the tall fencing.

The mayor declared a state of emergency.

No matter whom you asked, the event only proved their point.

The emergency order chastised the campers for "activities [that] include but are not limited to fires, explosions, public alcohol and drug use, violence and threats of violence, and defacing and damaging public and private property."

The anchor-outs, as Robbie put it, wondered why, after the city had spent almost half a million dollars on what it claimed were measures to protect and manage the camp, were there no fire extinguishers on site? It simply didn't make sense.

Not long after, as the encampment dwindled to little more than a dozen people, anger with the company contracted to ensure the campers' safety only grew when at least ten residents claimed to a *Pacific Sun* reporter that some of its employees "did drugs on the job" and in one case allegedly entered into a sexual relationship with an unhoused woman.

The accusations were never substantiated, and city officials declined to comment to the *Sun*. A representative from the company's public relations firm told the paper that the company had investigated the claims and did not find "any of the misconduct allegations to be true."

For the next months this back-and-forth continued. Then in early August, the city announced that it had reached an agreement

with the anchor-outs: each remaining camper, and a dozen or so former campers, about thirty in total, would receive an $18,000 settle-
ment. In exchange, they signed away any right to housing from the
city of Sausalito and agreed to leave the encampment, which would
be permanently closed.

A week later, it was gone.

IN THE SHORT TERM, ABOUT A THIRD of the thirty settlement recipients
purchased a vehicle to live in, while another third moved hundreds
of miles away to temporary housing near Lake Tahoe, still in search
of a permanent roof over their heads. The remainder either bought a
boat or stayed in a hotel room as they competed for housing vouchers
and sought out affordable living situations.

Peter and Jeff, in deference to their longevity as anchor-outs,
were allowed to return to their boats for the next three years, when
the entire anchorage would be cleared. John, for his part, moved to
Oakland while he was getting treatment for throat cancer. "I found
a place for as long as I can afford it, I guess," he would later comment
to reporters, estimating that he could last until the end of 2022.
In his lifetime on Richardson Bay, the city and the RBRA, by his
count, had destroyed seven of his boats. Now, with the encampment
gone, he said: "The whole community's been shattered—the whole
tradition, the whole legacy—and just been thrown to the wolves."

All told, the camp survived only a month or so longer than its
founder, Daniel, who had created Camp Cormorant in Dunphy
Park a year and a half earlier as a safe harbor for those who were
forced off the water or otherwise found themselves with nowhere
else to go.

Before his death that June, at eighty-four, he recorded a goodbye
message for his community: "Jesus Christ. Father, Son, and Holy

Ghost," he said, making the sign of the cross. "This moment is ab-solutely the greatest moment of my entire life. I'm eighty-four years old, and I can only say: I've never had the opportunity to feel this grateful. Since our Father has given me everything, I can give with you."

PART 5

THE CALM

2023

31

ON THE FOURTH OF JULY, IN 2023, I WENT TO DUNPHY PARK, HOPING TO watch the fireworks with the last of the anchor-outs.

Various estimates put the number of live-aboards that the RBRA and Sausalito police had been unable to evict at about forty, roughly 20 percent of the population at its peak a decade earlier. However, their days on the water were numbered: the BCDC had announced that local governments had to clear the remaining residents within three years.

On the Fourth in years past, the anchor-outs all milled about tables of food provided by local residents. This year, the day was overcast, and the only anchor-out I found was Peter, sitting barefoot in the grass, listening to a speaker playing in his backpack. Earlier, he said, there had been a bigger party. But it was nothing like years ago.

How are you? I asked him.

"Having a good day," he shouted over a metal guitar riff. He walked me over to a nearby picnic table and told me he'd spent his monthly check to feed his congregation. On the table were packs of hot dogs, buns, mustard, ketchup, and some tipped-over beers that had already been enjoyed.

I noted how much Sausalito had changed in the past few years.

"Oh yeah," Peter said. "Hell and back." He was hoping to write it all down in an autobiography of his life and his teachings. "I'd like to write the book in one paragraph," he said. "The spelling is what screws you up."

I asked him if Doug had come by, since they once shared the congregation.

"Doug!" he laughed. "He disappeared *off the map.* He is just *south of the border.*"

What about Dream?

"Last I heard he was living in the Tenderloin."

The wind began to pick up as the sun fell, blowing plastic grocery bags off the table.

Peter looked down at the spread. He offered a meal like this to the unhoused once a week, at church. "It costs $150. By the time I add everything, it's almost more than my fixed income. The reason I can do it is I don't pay rent or a mortgage or taxes. I feed people." He couldn't really make sense of all that had happened: the crushing of boats, the demolitions of Camp Cormorant. All for eelgrass? He laughed and pulled off his straw hat. "My hat is made of eelgrass." Later, when the anchor-outs were packed on top of each other in the muddy, fenced-in Marinship Park encampment, the city complained that people had gotten more violent. "Well, I've never seen two anchor-outs duke it out in all the time I've been here. We were gentleman pirates. It was the unrighteous pirates"—he pointed at the hill—"against the righteous pirates. It was pirates against pirates."

Another bag tumbled onto the grass.

Did he want help cleaning some of this up?

"No," Peter said. "Most people just get in my way." He told me to watch after the food while he brought some of the larger stuff to his skiff. With that, the seventy-eight-year-old put a cooler on the handlebars of his bicycle and rode off, pedaling barefoot, his beard trailing behind him.

PETER WAS GONE FAR LONGER THAN I'd expected. As the sun set, I started to wonder about my obligation to the hot dogs. Then an anchor-out in a blue windbreaker named James approached me.

"Is this Peter's stuff?" he asked.

I told him that it was, explaining the situation.

He examined the table, noting that the grill and the charcoal would require several more trips for Peter, who we both agreed was not going to be inclined to let us help him carry anything. After a moment, James concluded: "I'm gonna go get him a cart to help him," and he walked off in the opposite direction as Peter, toward the 7-Eleven.

JAMES ALSO DISAPPEARED FOR A VERY long time. Now it was near dusk, and I was shivering. The fireworks would be set off across the water in San Francisco in only an hour. The park was almost completely empty, except for a couple looking out at the boats bobbing in the anchorage. I thought back to the anchor-outs I had first met in the park in 2015. Almost every one of them had died, disappeared, or moved away.

When James finally returned, he was rolling a black leather office chair that looked like an Eames, hardly used at all.

As Peter approached, he pointed to it and thanked James, needing no explanation. He noticed I was shivering and suggested we light up the grill. "I'm hungry, how about you? Let's eat some hot dogs. It's the Fourth of July!"

"Eat!" James told his friend. He turned to me: "Peter is the type of guy who always feeds other people and never himself eats."

Peter squirted lighter fluid onto the coals and put a few dogs on the flame.

"You're still cold?" he said, intent on emptying the entire bottle of lighter fluid. When the dogs were done, he put them in some buns and covered them in mustard and relish. Biting off half his hot dog, he looked at me. "Let's pray for a coat for you." He put his head down and closed his eyes for a good long minute as he asked God to bring me a coat.

At last, his prayer finished, he looked up. "Okay," he said, wiping a glob of mustard from his beard. He put the rest of the hot dog in his mouth and shouted: "Now I feel alive!"

I turned to James and asked him if he knew anything about where Dream was.

"I only saw Dream's last boat when it was crushed." Like Peter, he thought he remembered someone saying that Dream went off to the Tenderloin. But, James said, he also heard that he died.

LATER IN THE EVENING, I OFFERED to take them for pizza at Taste of Rome, where we could sit out on the back patio and watch the fireworks.

They both agreed, and we began to pack up. Peter told James to take the grill—he was done with it. James placed the still-hot grill on his leather rolling chair as we walked toward the park exit.

I told him the grill was burning the chair.

"Oh, that's okay," he said. "I don't want this anyway." He pushed the chair off down the path in the opposite direction.

Peter was groaning under the weight of his backpack.

I asked if I could carry it for him.

"No!"

You sure? I asked.

"When I say no, I mean no."

I apologized; sometimes, I told him, it was my impression that people refused help even if they wanted it.

He nodded. "That's true," he said. "James! You got any good weed?"

James handed him a joint.

"Okay!" he said after a few hits. "Now I can make it." He took another couple of steps and groaned. He slipped off his backpack. "You know what? I could use a little help."

THAT NIGHT WE SAT AROUND AT Taste of Rome, eating pizzas.

At one point, a few guys walked up. "Can we have some?" they asked. They were anchor-outs, or had been. In any case, they wouldn't be soon. They put down their giant backpacks and joined us.

One of them, a blond guy, mentioned a former anchor-out who had died recently. "Two of his sons brought him across the country. He got COVID."

Peter sighed.

"He died in an assisted living facility in a complex in Nevada."

The table quieted down.

"Was he cremated?" Peter asked.

"I don't know."

"I don't want to be cremated."

I started shivering again, and the blond guy looked across the table at me. "You don't have a coat?" he asked. He reached into his backpack and handed me a blue windbreaker. "I just found this today," he said. "You can keep it."

Peter looked at me and laughed gently, clasping his hands in prayer.

A few minutes later, the fireworks in San Francisco started.

"I'm surprised they are so good," James said as light shot through the night sky.

"Not bad, not bad," said Peter, his face lighting up with the flashes of blue and red in the sky. "But I usually watch them from a boat."

"*Those*," the blond guy said, "are the best seats in town."

The booms set off a distant car alarm.

"Remember what Frank Sinatra did when a car alarm went off?" Peter asked.

"What?"

"He shot it!"

The blond guy leaned back and sang into the night air: "He did it *mmmmyyyy way.*"

32

IT WAS NOT UNLIKELY THAT DREAM, OR ANY OTHER FORMER ANCHOR-OUT, would end up in the Tenderloin.

The neighborhood is situated south of Nob Hill, one of the city's wealthiest enclaves, and north of Market Street, the main thoroughfare. Despite its proximity to wealth, the Tenderloin—a relatively small forty-block neighborhood in the fifty-square-mile metropolis—contains about 3,800 unhoused people, nearly half of all those without housing in San Francisco. It first began attracting low-income residents in the early years after World War II, when many mostly white people across the country were abandoning inner cities and securing cheap mortgages from the federal government and friendly banks to buy homes in the suburbs. Today 93 percent of the Tenderloin's 33,000 inhabitants don't own their homes, and about one-third of them live below the federal poverty line. Citywide, the median household income is almost $80,000; in the Tenderloin, it is $24,000. For the low-income residents of the Tenderloin, there are almost seven times the number of alcohol stores per square mile as in the whole of San Francisco, and not a single grocery store. By night, the entryways to the stores are lined with cardboard, providing makeshift overnight homes for the thousands of unhoused people.

On a cool evening later that July, I walked around the neighborhood to ask after Dream. None of the shop owners and passersby I spoke to recognized my description of him. One man I met had just moved back to the city from Thailand, but someone had dented his van overnight and now he hoped to save up enough to leave again. Another, a woman I sat next to on the bus, was giving the bus driver overly detailed directions.

The bus driver started to laugh, and I joined in.

What? she asked.

I told her she sounded like a New Yorker giving a tourist directions to the subway.

"I'm a schoolteacher," she explained.

I asked if she lived in the neighborhood.

She looked out the window and sighed. "In a shelter."

Even though she had a full-time job?

She had lost her place and couldn't find anything in the city she could afford on her salary. "It's just for now," she said, before I stepped off the bus.

It was night, and my phone was dead. I passed a young guy, maybe twenty, lying down on some flattened boxes in an entryway. He was clean-shaven with a scar on his face that looked like it had been there a while.

We made eye contact, and he asked me where I was going.

My hotel, I told him, though I couldn't seem to find it.

He asked which one it was, but I couldn't remember the name. "Is it nice?"

I told him a room was about $60 a night.

He laughed. "It's this way." He stood up and started walking with me. He wasn't following me, he explained. It was just time for him to move anyway; his spot wasn't safe to sleep at anymore. "You think I am homeless, don't you?" he said.

It had crossed my mind.

"I'm not homeless, man." He told me he had a home, but it was in Nashville.

What brought him out here?

He said he'd followed his girlfriend, but it didn't work out.

That sort of thing rarely does, I said. There were entire Amtrak lounge cars full of people giving it a shot every day, so it was nothing to feel too down about.

"But I sold my car," he said. And now he was out of money.

We passed a bar that was still open, named Aces, and I asked him if he wanted to sit down for a bit. As he sipped a beer, he told me it was more complicated than the car being sold or him being out of money. His parents were still alive, and they could probably help him. But he'd gotten into a fight with his father. It was a bad fight. Starting to cry, he was talking fast and getting hard to understand. It sounded like the fight happened because he'd been on heroin at the time. I wasn't sure that was what he said, but I didn't clarify, because it didn't really matter.

I'm sure your parents still want you back home, I said. Whatever happened, they still would rather you were with them than alone out here, sleeping in a doorway.

"I know, yeah. They would—"

So why not call them?

"No," he told me. He was just going to stay. He shook his head, like even he couldn't explain why.

33

DURING THAT EVENING WITH THE GUY FROM NASHVILLE, I'D FOUND OUT that the bartender at Aces lived in Sausalito. So a few days later, I went back, stopping by around noon.

He and his partner, he said, paid about $3,000 a month for an apartment in Marin County. It wasn't cheap, but it was better than San Francisco.

I asked what he thought about the anchor-outs.

He really didn't follow that situation very much. He knew a few of the guys on the waterfront, but that was it.

I told him I was looking for one named Dream. He was an odd guy, a former clown. He had a Southern California accent. Come to think of it, I wasn't quite sure why he had lived all those years on the anchorage. It occurred to me that "Why?" was never a question Dream answered about anything, at least not to me. Everything just *was* with him. He was Innate's brother, after all, so he too had gotten an inheritance. For whatever reason, he had never left Richardson Bay. Until now.

Anyway, I told the bartender, he was in a wheelchair. He had long hair and leathery skin, cured by decades of sun and ocean air. He was in his sixties, but he looked older, probably more than I remembered, even from a year ago.

"Dream?" the bartender said. "No."

But, he explained, Aces was at the top edge of the Tenderloin. "We only get some of the essence." An anchor-out would probably be blocks farther inside, where thousands of men and women without homes would spend the night, in the center of one of the wealthiest cities in America.

There could be a Dream in there, he told me, pointing southward out the window, toward somewhere lower down.

34

IN LATE NOVEMBER, A FEW MONTHS AFTER I RETURNED TO NEW YORK, MY phone rang.

"Hey, brother," Innate said.

We hadn't spoken in a while. Though we had scheduled a few calls, they always fell through. For one thing, Innate's job at the weed farm was demanding: he rose before dawn each day, inspected buds until late afternoon, and went to bed just after dinner. On weekends, he struggled to balance the tending of his crops with the hunting of squirrels and the occasional afternoon spent with distant neighbors. One Saturday not long before he called, I texted the latest of his ever-changing phone numbers to see if he was free. "Sorry, pal," he replied the next day. "I ate some shrooms."

I was happy we finally got a chance to talk, I told him.

He said that he left his job. It turned out, he reflected, that even the world of corporatized marijuana cultivation was too corporate for him: "The funny thing was, I cut my hair and ended up getting a job growing pot." It was all right, he said; his heart was never really in the nine-to-five lifestyle anyway. "I got the job because Melissa and I split up and I had ended up with a lot of debt." Now that he'd moved past the breakup, at least financially, he wanted no boss but the weather.

What would he do now?

"Next April, I plan on planting hemp. Not the CBD stuff— the productive stuff. I'll be essentially growing bamboo. My first product I want to try is heating pellets. You don't need a permit for that . . ." he said, trailing off in thought. His end of the line went quiet.

I asked if something was on his mind.

"Say, by chance, did you get any information about my brother Dream?"

I told him what I'd heard on the waterfront: that some anchor-outs spoke of rumors that Dream was living in San Francisco, in the Tenderloin, and that others told of a grimmer fate.

"I don't know," Innate said. His siblings had been looking for Dream for a year. "Here is the story I heard: He was hanging out with some people. He got up to go to the store to get a pack of ciga-rettes, and no one has heard from him since. I think it was foul play."

Why did he think someone would hurt his brother?

"I just don't perceive my brother telling people, 'I'm going to the store,' and disappearing. He didn't have the resources. He'd spent his inheritance gambling with Bo. Dream enjoyed being in the spot-light in the community. Why would someone like that just walk? It doesn't make sense."

By Innate's reckoning, the trouble all began about ten years ear-lier. One afternoon, while Innate was on his boat, Dream rowed up to him in a panic. The police were chasing him. The officers followed Dream onto the deck, tackled him, and handcuffed him. Innate then said that when Dream arrived at the jail, officers roughed him up. The reason for the harsh treatment, Innate claimed, was that the police had incorrectly identified his brother as a man with a very similar name who was wanted for attempted murder. When they re-alized the error, he said, they released Dream without charges. "They confused my brother for him. They beat him up in the cell and then realized they had the wrong guy. He's been targeted majorly since that day—because they fucked up big."

I told Innate I was surprised that, after all these years, I hadn't come across the case of another man named Richard Archer who was accused of murder in Marin County.

That was because his brother's name was Richard Dream Weaver, Innate said.

I knew that many anchor-outs, like Innate, changed their names on the water. But, I asked, didn't the state still know him as Richard Archer?

"No," Innate said. "Richard Dream Weaver. He changed that long ago because he was a clown. He was trying to cash a check some asshole wrote to Dream Weaver the Clown." It was just his brother's bad luck that a man in New Orleans wrote the check to him using almost the same name as another man who, decades later, across the country, would be a suspect in a drive-by shooting.

But, I asked, what about all the people who said they saw his brother in San Francisco?

"The only thing that I would ever get is: 'So-and-so said somebody saw him in the city.' So I would ask, 'Well, can you get me in touch with so-and-so?'" Every trail Innate followed led nowhere. "When you put it all together, it leaves one rather boggled." Still, Innate conceded that these were only theories, assembled from afar, alone in the Arizona desert. "There is the reality that both of my brothers have disappeared for a number of years of my life."

Innate and I spoke often on the phone in late 2023. One afternoon he blurted out: "What happened to Dream? What happened to him?" There was a time not so long ago when Innate would have been able to find the answer, to follow the rumors across the water, to arrive at the truth. But those days were gone. Sausalito, he told me, had scattered the anchor-outs to the wind, and with them went their relationships, their obligations, their owed favors, their traditions. The elders who commanded respect and information had died or disappeared. Now he doubted he'd ever figure out what happened to Dream. "There are probably just maybe five people left who know what's what." Now, he said, "the facts are elusive. The stories are just stories."

After we hung up, I decided to reach out to the anchor-outs I'd known over the years, to see if there was anyone who knew anything about what happened to Dream Weaver. But as I looked through my notebook, I realized that almost everyone was gone: Larry, Diane, Bo, Rose, Innate, Melissa, Daniel, John, Jim, and Doug had all died or been forced to move away. The few I knew who were left either changed their number or didn't reply.

Eventually, however, I got ahold of Robbie.

"I heard from a guy named Nic that he found him living out in San Francisco," he told me, and passed along Nic's number. Nic, I learned, was Nic Mosher, a documentary filmmaker who'd been making a movie about Peter.

"Well, you found him," Nic said when I called, sharing the name of the shop outside of which Dream had pitched his tent. "He spends his days crocheting really intricate sweaters. And he uses the money to buy coffee at Starbucks so he can use their bathroom."

How did you find him? I asked.

"My friend lived nearby," Nic explained. The friend knew Nic was filming an anchor-out and, when he saw Dream, was struck by how he looked like one: the strange hat, the long hair and beard, that certain way they've learned to carry themselves after surviving on the water for all those decades, weathering vengeful gulls and harbormasters, being laughed at for claiming the world was out to get them until one day it did. And so it was as simple as that: Dream, presumed lost, unfindable, had been found by someone who wasn't even looking.

I called Innate with the news.

"That's awesome," he said, pausing. "He's doing all right."

I asked him what he made of his brother disappearing.

"I couldn't blame him," he told me. "A lot of the old-timers passed away. The anchorage—everyone is just drifting now." Innate wanted something more stable for his brother and hoped he'd move out to the desert in Arizona. Together, they could grow hemp for commercial production. Or, if Dream didn't want to grow hemp,

Innate didn't mind doing it all himself, letting his brother just live on the property, crocheting his days away, as he'd loved to do since their grandmother had taught him the cable stitch as a child. "I want him to have a safe place to retreat to instead of being on the side of the road. He could still live in a tent if he wants," Innate said. "My intention is to provide love for him."

Did he think Dream would move to the desert? I asked. In the last six years, Innate had built a life on his dry mesa: a grove had blossomed from the saplings he found in a hospital parking lot, and his garden flourished with the fruit and vegetable plants he'd bought using food stamps at Walmart. He had fresh clean water, an old pickup truck, an ATV, a solar cooker, and a hot shower. Dream was welcome to all of it. But it was a solitary life—forty acres of isolation, cold at night, sweltering in the day. He had neighbors, and he even liked a few of them, but it was nothing like Dream's long years of life on the water.

Innate thought about it some more and sighed. "I don't know," he said. "If a message could drift his way that I love him . . . we can take it from there."

A FEW DAYS LATER, NIC SENT me a video he'd shot of Dream by his tent in San Francisco. He was wearing a red coat, sitting in his wheelchair, flashing what had become a toothless grin. Into the camera, he told the story that Innate had been searching for—the story of his last days on Richardson Bay and of what happened in the years since he vanished from the waterfront: what his life had been like when he lost his boat, when they bulldozed the first encampment, when they evicted the residents from the second encampment, when he wound up in the wheelchair, when he vanished from the bay and arrived in San Francisco:

"My name is Richard Dream Weaver, and I am the real Richard

Dream Weaver," he declared.* "I was living on a boat in Richardson Bay for twenty-four years—actually five different boats. They crushed all five, one at a time. The last one was after the pandemic hit. They crushed it. That's the way that they were, you know: politics as usual in Marin.

"In April 2020, I was visiting with my niece at this homeless camp on the shoreline right at Dunphy Park, and I was walking along the pathway going home, and a tent blew up and it blew me up. And the guy that was inside the tent that collapsed on him was all on fire. I ran back into the fire to pull him out. He was in an easy chair. The chair was melting on him. Everything was melting on him. The only thing that didn't melt on his body was his butt and part of his thigh where he was sitting down. Everything else was burnt. But I saved him. I took him out. I started throwing propane tanks and butane cans out of the area that was in the flames because children at the campsite were coming to see the fire.

"I don't have fear in my body. I don't have a fear of anything really. I just did the right thing: he was on fire, he was a human being, and he was my friend, and I saved him. He had a heart attack at the parking lot, and so the ambulance, when they arrived, they shocked him back to life again and put him on a gurney. They didn't even attend to me until after they were done with him. They put me in the ambulance, and they took me to the hospital.

"He was on a gurney with 85 percent of his body burnt third degree, and he was right in front of me in the hallway of the hospital. They're announcing us on the PA system, saying no patients will be admitted until 8:00. There was an overhanging clock in the hallway. It said 7:15. In the meantime, my feet were burnt, and they were hurting really bad. I could only imagine what Ray was going through. At a quarter till, he had a stroke and so they had to attend

---

* I have shortened and lightly edited Dream's account for clarity and length.

to him. They took him away. They gave me a little roll of gauze and a small little sampling tube of some ointment.

"Fortunately for me, a friend saw me at the front of the hospital and took me back with them to the homeless camp. So I stayed. They put me into what they called the supply tent. I was in this supply tent for a little while until they were coming in there and they were smoking their speed and they were shooting up. And do you know what? Over the course of time, I became quite favorable to the speed as well, because I was in the atmosphere. It was affecting me. Finally, I started smoking it—worst thing you can do, all right?

"At any rate, that was after the fire. Months later on. I was barely walking to the bathroom at that time. My feet were burnt. I was having to poop in a bucket, and people were having to empty my poop bucket for me for a while. But after I could walk on my feet and stumble around, I fell and I broke my hip. They took me to a hospital. The hospital said: 'No, he's not coming in here.'

"Now mind you, I am a good patient. I have a good heart. I'm a peaceful, loving individual. People pass me by all the time and say, 'Richard, I love you,' because they feel the love that I have for them. And it's amazing to me, because here I am now on the streets of San Francisco and they're still loving me."

Why do you think the hospital wanted to get rid of you so bad? Nic asked.

"Well, I think I know. I've been one of the, uh, 'heavy hitters' out there on Richardson Bay. For twenty-some-odd years now they've been trying to get rid of me, they don't want me anywhere near anyone with a head that can think because I will fill them full of information, and then they will stop capitulating to the authorities. On the water, especially in Richardson Bay, it is a very unique place in the world. It's open to the ocean, therefore it is an open, navigable water and unregulated by any country. It belongs to the ocean. It does not belong to Marin County or all those people that want a piece of the pie.

"I was off my boat now when I fell and broke my hip. They immediately sent me over to another hospital, where they operated on me. They told me, 'You should be able to walk within a few days.' That was in July of 2020. Here we are in 2023. I'm still in this freaking wheelchair. Sometime while my hip's been broken, that's when they crushed my boat and made me homeless. If it weren't for the fact that I couldn't walk, I would still be on my boat. They're trying to cover up everything that they can because they don't want me to have a multimillion-dollar lawsuit. Everybody's telling me, 'Oh, you got it made. You're going to be rich.'

"No, I don't have it made.

"I have no identity. I can't even verify who I am. It took me a year to get a California identification card. Once I got it, I went down to the Social Security Department. They said, 'We don't accept that. You have to have a real ID, a birth certificate, a passport.'

"I started smoking meth for a couple of days, then I switched to crack cocaine. Now here's why I switched to crack cocaine. It gives you a similar high as the speed, but it's a mental addiction. It is not a physical addiction. It got me off of the physical addiction. And then they started putting fentanyl into the crack, so I stopped. And that was about fourteen months ago, not too long ago. The people in this neighborhood have chosen to rally behind me. The people feed me. I can't go hungry in this town.

"At my age—I'm now sixty-six—I have a lot of life experience, they call it. I've done a lot of things that I've overcome. I will overcome this too."

Dream told Nic to hold up a piece he was in the process of crocheting.

"You can't even follow it because I have no pattern. I just make it up," Dream said. "It's going to be a cormorant when it's finished, and he's going to be standing with a yellow sun. He's going to be standing on a pylon in the ocean, behind him, with a red-back, red-sky background."

When the anchor-outs were first evicted from the water, they named their camp after the cormorant. They drew it on flags that they hoisted above their battered, muddy tents. Now, after everything was over, here was Dream on the other side of the bay, crocheting the cormorant again and again into sweaters.

When Nic asked Dream about the bird's significance to the anchor-outs, Dream explained that "the cormorant was an endangered species. It was being hunted out. It was dying off, and it had infested the Bay Bridge in San Francisco—the old Bay Bridge. All along the bridge they had nests. So when they were building the new Bay Bridge, they couldn't just destroy the whole of the old Bay Bridge, because it was nesting ground for a protected species—the cormorant. So they left parts of the bridge up so the cormorants could be there, and then they included areas in the new bridge that would attract the cormorants. Some of them came, but most of them liked their old place and just hung out there.

"But at any rate, the cormorant won't let you go near it in the first place. If you get one hundred feet from it, it's going to take off because they don't trust you. You're a man or a woman, and it don't trust humans at all. But it stands on pylons and on rocks and high places—high places because it's not a very good flier. It flies better underwater than it does in the sky. It dries itself out in the sun, and it warms its body up, and then it dives down and catches more fish. It flies underwater real fast, and it can turn on a dime."

Dream Weaver grinned.

"You know what it eats?" he asked. "Eelgrass."

A FEW DAYS LATER, MY PHONE rang.

"I just got a call from my brother!" Innate shouted. They had spoken for about ten minutes. Extracting Dream from the Bay Area would be difficult, since Dream was convinced he was being watched. Innate shouldn't call, Dream said. Instead, they could work out a system of code words to text. That way they could figure out a secret location for the extraction, one that would leave no paper trail.

After the call, Innate took his truck to a mechanic to see if it could make the trip. It was a tough call, the man said. If he took it really easy, it might survive, but taking the trip might also be the end of it. To Innate, it didn't matter. He had saved $1,000, and one way or another he'd get his brother. "People have capitalism all wrong," he told me. "It's only bad if you abuse it." He recounted a time, long ago, when he was riding around with a wealthy man who hung out on the waterfront. The man pulled up to a red light and noticed a woman who looked miserable and tired, soliciting drivers at the intersection. He reached into his wallet, pulled out a $50 bill, and gave it to Innate. "Just hand this to her," he said. When Innate rolled down the window and gave the woman the money, she walked off, abandoning the intersection. "That," Innate told me, "is capitalism in a healthy form."

He estimated it might take a few months to get his brother to Arizona.

I asked him if he was nervous about the two of them living alone in the desert.

No, he said. "When you get pushed hard, amazing things happen."

In some ways, I said, with Melissa gone, with Dream coming to live with him in Arizona, I imagined it felt like an ending to his connection with Richardson Bay.

"You know, I often miss sleeping on the water," Innate said. The waves had rocked him to sleep, and while there was space between his neighbors, they were still close enough to cook dinner together, to talk about their lives before the anchorage and their hopes for their lives after it. Nevertheless, the life he was now living—on the patch of cool high Arizona mesa that he owned and had built on, with a hot shower and a garden he had planted, and soon with the brother he used to sled down the hill with on cardboard boxes—was a life that eight years before, on the first day I met Innate and Dream in Dunphy Park, they could only have wished they had.

The sun was shining that day in April 2015, and the anchor-outs were scattered about, their homes bobbing safely at a distance. Bo was listening to his radio on the bench by the bocce ball court, and Jeff, dressed in white, was handing out flyers for the Jubilee on the beach. Off on Liberty Dock, Larry and Diane were with Handsome Harry. Innate and Dream, meanwhile, were standing under an old tree discussing how, with the help of neodymium magnets and some plans they found on the internet at the Sausalito library, they might be able to create a water heater.

"Take twenty-four magnets and spin them at 3,000 RPM," Innate said. "One guy took that concept, and he put it on a spindle, with rectangular magnets. And he ran copper tubing from stoves, like a manifold. And he's getting eighty degrees of constant hot water. These guys are using industrial motors. But you can get a computer—a DVD motor—to spin at 4,500 RPM."

"Yeah," Dream said, after mulling over his brother's plan. "But that's just spinning a DVD. How much does a DVD weigh?"

Innate nodded. "I could replace the aluminum with plastic?"

"Plastic will melt. Kevlar maybe."

After some debate, they both agreed Kevlar would be difficult to obtain. And on further consideration, so would all the magnets, and the motor.

Innate sighed. "I just want some way to get under some hot water."

"Or a cup of coffee."

Oh well, they agreed. They'd think of something, someday.

They walked over to the shoreline to brainstorm. The day was quiet and the harbormaster was in his station. It would be years before the storms and fires and floods and sewage; before the BCDC was audited and the Transition Plan was put in place; before the harbormaster and police and city council washed them all away. That day, tall sails flapped in the wind as birds circled above their beat-up, imperfect homes. There were the gulls who'd always been there, and the pelicans too. There were the crows who'd just recently made their way west, and there were the terns who, now and then, were known to drop downward, in pointed free fall, plunging beneath the surface of the water to spear a herring or, if they were hungry enough, to take a fish from another bird. The practice was accepted by the other animals in the harbor and, as far as we knew, it always had been: a concession, perhaps, that desperation is its own hard-enough life.

For a while, I couldn't hear what Dream and Innate were saying to one another as their words blew away into the wind. Then Dream began to sing the theme song to *Felix the Cat*, the old cartoon they had watched together as children all those decades ago in San Diego:

"*Felix the cat, the wonderful wonderful cat*"—Innate laughed and bopped back and forth as he joined Dream—"*You'll never know what he does next, so don't even try to take a guess . . .*"

EPILOGUE
2024

DISAPPEARANCE, THROUGH FORCE OR TRICKERY, IS OFTEN THE OBJECTIVE of policies aimed at unhoused communities. This objective is not unique to Sausalito. One can find it anywhere. Thousands of cities across the United States bus unhoused people out of town, with no means to return. They are regularly pushed out of West Palm Beach, Denver, Portland, and, as identified by an eighteen-month *Guardian* investigation, at least a dozen other urban areas with large concentrated unhoused communities. In New York City, for example, leaders have been characteristically unsubtle for decades: Rudy Giuliani, Michael Bloomberg, and Bill de Blasio, each of a different political party, spent their tenures as mayor buying one-way tickets out of town for those living on the streets, shipping them as far away as South Africa. And though the city's current mayor, Eric Adams, attempted to couple his plan to clear all twenty-nine known encampments in the city's subway system with another pledge to construct new shelters, it is nevertheless the case that, in 2022, when more than 470 people were arrested for being "outstretched" in stations and on trains, his administration was decreasing funding for homeless services amid a budget shortfall. Adams probably would have preferred to find homes in the city for all those New Yorkers huddled together each night on urine-soaked concrete platforms, but it is clear that their eviction, not their well-being, was his priority. And it is also possible, though perhaps not plausible, that the mayor was sincere when he made this pledge to build more shelters. But having made it so early in his tenure, he had yet to grasp the century and a half of hurdles his forebears in City Hall had placed in his way.

In Sausalito's case, however, such a possibility seems far more remote: with its shortage of housing stock, its median income of $76,000, and its years of opposition to even adjusting its zoning ordinances to *allow* for the construction of shelters, could anyone attending city council meetings between 2015 and 2023 really have believed that forcing hundreds of anchor-outs off the water and crushing their boats would lead them to find housing in the community? It is true that, upon the closure of the final iteration of the encampment, a few dozen residents received $18,000 to secure housing and a handful more of the old-timers, like Jeff and Peter, were allowed to stay in the bay until 2026. But what then? Where is everyone supposed to go?

At book's end, I'm afraid that I'm no closer to answering that question. But the story of the anchor-outs should make us wonder: Why does it ever have to be asked at all?

THE LAST TIME I SPOKE TO Jeff, in the spring of 2024, I asked him what happened to most of the anchor-outs.

He didn't know. They were just gone.

Of course, *something* had happened to them. No doubt that something, for many of them, had been as exhausting and painful as the past few years of Dream's life. One can only hope they, too, have a brother with a garden in the desert where they can rest awhile.

I reminded Jeff of how he used to talk of the Jubilee.

"Oh, don't put too much into that," he said.

Why did he stop talking about it?

"Everyone who needed to hear about it heard about it." As conditions worsened on the water, the anchor-outs kept asking when it would arrive, but at some point it stopped making sense to bring it up.

So what about him? Where would he go when his number came up on the anchorage?

"There is only one place."

What is it?

"Jerusalem."

Was he really planning to sail his boat from Richardson Bay all the way to the Levant?

"Yes, I'll go to Gaza. I'll bring food to people."

But wouldn't it be dangerous, sailing two open oceans all alone in a tiny boat? Thrashed by waves and storms, carried along by unpredictable currents with no one to help him if he lost his way?

He let out a peaceful sigh. "Oh yes," he said. "It is."

ACKNOWLEDGMENTS

I am grateful to many people for this book. First and foremost, to the anchor-outs: Innate—the Virgil of this project—as well as Melissa, Dream, Bo, Jeff, Rose, Peter, James, Lotus, Tim, Richard, Sydney, Chappy, Daniel, Angel, Larry, Diane, Keven, John, Jim, Lisa, Doug, and Robbie. I'm lucky to have known them. I'm also very grateful to those who helped make this book happen: to Winston Choi-Schagrin and Grace Ross for their encouragement at the start, and to my agent, Stephanie Steiker, as well as, at Dey Street, to Chelsea Herrera and David Wienir, and to my editor Anna Montague. I appreciate the time and effort they all spent shaping this story. This project began as an article in *Harper's Magazine*, and I'm in debt to Stephanie McFeeters and Matt Sherrill for their work on it, as their insights proved invaluable. Also invaluable to the book was the research contributions of Nora Sawyer at the Sausalito Public Library and the video of Dream filmed by Nic Mosher, which he generously provided me. Many of my reporting trips relied on the hospitality of old friends in the Bay Area: Jaeah Lee, Cameron Bird, and Vince Romanin. I'm also thankful for the thoughts and guidance offered as the story took shape by my friends Hasan Altaf, Marisa Nakasone, Ryann Liebenthal, Saki Knafo, and Maxwell Strachan, and for the mentorship and helping hands given to me early in my career by Greg Boustead and Steve Silberman. For all of their support, I'm lucky for my parents, Joyce and Emil Babyak; my sister, brother-in-law, and niece—Mary, Itai, and Ayala Pinkoviezky; and, for more than I can express, Bindu Bansinath.

NOTES

Introduction

2 *US Congress declared:* 33 Code of Federal Regulations § 110.126a (San Francisco Bay, CA), https://www.law.cornell.edu/cfr/text/33/110.126a.

2 *municipalities of the bay consolidated:* "Richardson Bay Joint Exercise of Powers Agreement," July 16, 1985, https://rbra.ca.gov/files/d3fbec5af/1985-07-16+_JPA+fully+ex.pdf.

2 *They passed ordinances:* Richardson Bay Regional Agency, "Ordinance No. 87-1: An Ordinance of the Richardson Bay Regional Agency, State of California, Establishing Rules and Regulations for Anchoring and Mooring in Richardson Bay and Belvedere Cove," July 9, 1987, https://rbra.ca.gov/files/0709e0662/0rd87-1.pdf.

4 *recognize it when it comes:* Edmund Love, *Subways Are for Sleeping* (Harcourt, Brace, 1957), 9.

4 *600,000 people:* US Department of Housing and Urban Development, "The 2023 Annual Homelessness Assessment Report (AHAR) to Congress," December 2023, https://www.huduser.gov/portal/sites/default/files/pdf/2023-AHAR-Part-1.pdf.

4 *bring the miracle:* Love, *Subways Are for Sleeping,* 9.

5 *grew by 57 percent:* US Department of Housing and Urban Development, "The 2015 Annual Homelessness Assessment Report (AHAR) to Congress," November 2015, https://www.huduser.gov/portal/sites/default/files/pdf/2015-AHAR-Part-1.pdf.

5 *number of unhoused people:* San Francisco Human Services Agency, with Applied Survey Research, "2009 San Francisco Homeless Count and Survey," https://hsh.sfgov .org/wp-content/uploads/2017/02/HomelessCountFINALReportSF2009.pdf; Applied Survey Research, "2015 San Francisco Homeless Point-in-Time Count and Survey," https://hsh.sfgov.org/wp-content/uploads/2016/06/2015-San-Francisco-Homeless -Count-Report_0-1.pdf.

6 *median home value:* State of California, Employment Development Department, "Historical Data for Median Price of Existing Homes Sold in Marin County," https:// labormarketinfo.edd.ca.gov/cgi/databrowsing/localAreaProfileQSMoreResult.asp?me nuChoice=localAreaPro&criteria=property+values&categoryType=economicindicato rs&geogArea=0604000041&area=Marin+County&timeseries=property+valuesTime Series.

6 *45 percent of longtime employees:* "Affordable Housing: Time for Collaboration in Marin," 2021–2022 Marin County Civil Grand Jury, June 24, 2022, https://www .marincounty.org/-/media/files/departments/gj/reports-responses/2021-22/afford able-housing--time-for-collaboration-in-marin.pdf?la=en.

6 *increased 36 percent:* County of Marin Health and Human Services, "Marin County 2013 Point in Time Count Comprehensive Report Findings," https://www.marinhhs

.org/sites/default/files/files/servicepages/2013_09/2013_point_in_time_count_full _report.pdf.

6 *epidemic of homelessness:* US Department of Housing and Urban Development, "The 2023 Annual Homelessness Assessment Report (AHAR) to Congress."

6 *as of 2024:* "2024 Point-in-Time-Count," San Francisco Department of Homeless Services, https://hsh.sfgov.org/about/research-and-reports/pit/.

7 *one 2020 study:* Deborah K. Padgett, "Homelessness, Housing Instability and Mental Health: Making the Connections," *BJPsych Bulletin* 44, no. 5 (October 2020): 197–201, https://www.ncbi.nlm.nih.gov/pmc/articles/PMC7525583/.

Chapter 1

14 *formed the Richardson Bay Regional Agency (RBRA):* "Richardson Bay Joint Exercise of Powers Agreement," July 16, 1985, https://rbra.ca.gov/files/d3fbec5af/1985-07-16 +_JPA+fully+ex.pdf.

14 *At the state level:* San Francisco Bay Conservation and Development Commission, "The McAteer-Petris Act: As Amended Through the 1995 Legislative Session," California Government Code 66600–66682, The_McAteer-Petris_Act-_as_amended_through _1995.pdf (bayplanningcoalition.org).

16 *recent Supreme Court ruling:* Lozman v. City of Riviera Beach, 568 U.S. 115 (2013).

Chapter 2

20 *issue of rezoning:* State of California, Department of Housing and Community Development, "Senate Bill 2: Local Planning and Approval for Emergency Shelters and Transition and Supportive Housing," May 7, 2008, https://www.hcd.ca.gov /community-development/housing-element/housing-element-memos/docs/sb2-me mo050708.pdf.

20 *council once again gathered:* City of Sausalito, "Sausalito City Council Regular Meeting," February 24, 2015, https://sausalito.granicus.com/player/clip/199?view_id=6& meta_id=23798&redirect=true.

23 *home price in Sausalito:* State of California, Employment Development Department, "Historical Data for Median Price of Existing Homes Sold in Marin County," https:// labormarketinfo.edd.ca.gov/cgi/databrowsing/localAreaProfileQSMoreResult.asp?me nuChoice=localAreaPro&criteria=property+values&categoryType=economicindicato rs&geogArea=0604000041&area=Marin+County&timeseries=property+valuesTime Series.

Chapter 3

29 *two-thousand-year-old caravan city:* Anne Barnard, "Jihadists May Have Wrecked an Ancient Iraqi Site," *New York Times*, March 7, 2015, https://www.nytimes.com /2015/03/08/world/middleeast/jihadists-may-have-wrecked-an-ancient-iraqi-site.html.

31 *largest funders of the RBRA:* "Richardson Bay Joint Exercise of Powers Agreement," July 16, 1985, https://rbra.ca.gov/files/d3fbec5af/1985-07-16+_JPA+fully+ex.pdf.

32 *deemed a* vessel: 2007 US Code, Title 1, Chapter 1, "Rules of Construction," § 3— "'Vessel' as including all means of water transportation."

32 *"Jonah inside the whale":* Burks v. American River Transp. Co., 679 F.2d 69 (5th Cir., 1982), https://casetext.com/case/burks-v-american-river-transp-co-2.

32   *"To state the obvious":* Lozman v. City of Riviera Beach, 568 U.S. 115 (5, 2013). https://supreme.justia.com/cases/federal/us/568/115/

Chapter 4

40   *The Arques family:* Larry Clinton, "Godfather of the Waterfront," Sausalito Historical Society, December 1, 2021, https://www.sausalitohistoricalsociety.com/2021-columns/2021/11/26/godfather-of-the-waterfront.

42   *chemical toilets: Fresh Garlic* 2, no. 2 (1977).

42   *the* Clamshell: *Fresh Garlic* 3, no. 2 (1977).

47   *only news stories:* Mark Prado, "Death Near Sausalito Park Is Called 'Suspicious' by Police," *Marin Independent Journal*, May 1, 2015, https://www.marinij.com/2015/05/01/death-near-sausalito-park-is-called-suspicious-by-police/.

Chapter 5

53   *causes of death:* Kevin Mullen, "Homicide in San Francisco, 1849–2003," The Ohio State University College of Arts and Sciences, Criminal Justice Research Center, https://cjrc.osu.edu/research/interdisciplinary/hvd/united-states/san-francisco.

53   *brig named the* Euphemia: "The Prison Ship 'Euphemia,' *Found SF*, historical essay based on an article by James P. Delgado, *California History* (Fall 1978), https://www.foundsf.org/index.php?title=The_Prison_Ship_%27Euphemia%27.

53   *"What is this liberty":* Learned Hand, "The Spirit of Liberty," speech delivered in celebration of I Am an American Day 1944, Foundation for Independent Rights and Expression, https://superiorcourt.maricopa.gov/media/brxnkvvu/the-spirit-of-liberty_-speech-by-judge-learned-hand.pdf.

Chapter 6

63   *the members convened:* City of Sausalito, Sausalito City Council Regular Meeting, May 3, 2016, https://sausalito.granicus.com/player/clip/287?view_id=6&redirect=true.

66   *"killing his landlord":* Gary Klien, "Man Charged with Murdering Landlord with Crowbar Found Dead in Marin County Jail," *Mercury News*, April 28, 2015, https://www.mercurynews.com/2015/04/28/man-charged-with-murdering-landlord-with-a-crowbar-found-dead-in-marin-county-jail/.

Chapter 7

70   *"like a gold miner":* Dan Brekke, "Ale Ekstrom, Sausalito Anchor-Out and Independent Spirit, Dies at Age 78," KQED, July 29, 2015, https://www.kqed.org/news/10621093/ale-ekstrom-sausalito-anchor-out-and-independent-spirit-dies-at-age-78.

70   *candidates were fighting:* Aaron Blake, "The First Trump-Clinton Presidential Debate Transcript, Annotated," *Washington Post*, September 26, 2016, https://www.washingtonpost.com/news/the-fix/wp/2016/09/26/the-first-trump-clinton-presidential-debate-transcript-annotated/.

71   *living in San Francisco:* San Francisco Human Services Agency, with Applied Survey Research, "2017 San Francisco Homeless Count and Survey," https://hsh.sfgov.org/wp-content/uploads/2017/06/2017-SF-Point-in-Time-Count-General-FINAL-6.21.17.pdf.

74   *two million gallons:* "Southern Marin Sewers: Crack in the System," 2008–2009 Marin County Civil Grand Jury, May 5, 2009, https://www.marincounty.org/-/media/files /departments/gj/reports-responses/2008/southern_marin_sewers.pdf.

74   *Between 2011 and 2013:* "The Scoop on Marin County Sewer Systems: Part 1," 2013– 2014 Marin County Civil Grand Jury, June 16, 2014, https://www.parks.marincounty .org/-/media/files/departments/gj/reports-responses/2013/sewerscoopi.pdf.

75   *two-volume draft report:* "Environmental Impact Report for Waldo Point Harbor," Marin County, May 23, 1997.

75   *"clear and present danger":* Mark Prado, "Enforcement Takes Center Stage in Richardson Bay 'Anchor Out' Debate," *Marin Independent Journal,* April 15, 2016, https:// www.marinij.com/2016/04/15/enforcement-takes-center-stage-in-richardson-bay -anchor-out-debate/.

75   *decades-old city law:* "Ordinance No. 1108: An Ordinance of the City of Sausalito Amending Section 16.16.020 'Written Consent Required' of Chapter 16.16 'Moorage' of the Sausalito Municipal Code Relating to Overnight Moorage of Boats on City Waters," March 7, 1995, https://sausalito.granicus.com/MetaViewer.php?view_id=6& clip_id=125&meta_id=15566.

76   *story of the Houseboat Wars:* Jeff Costello, "Sausalito Houseboat War, 1971," *Anderson Valley Advertiser,* August 21, 2013, https://theava.com/archives/23500.

76   *inspector cited houseboats:* Jonah Owen Lamb, "Held Fast: How Renegade 'Squatters' Won Sausalito's Houseboat Wars," *SF Weekly,* September 16, 2015, https://www .sfweekly.com/archives/held-fast-how-renegade-squatters-won-sausalitos-houseboat -wars/article_7c308108-df4c-5e87-83a9-acc4c0b9090e.html.

Chapter 8

79   *"Bay or River?":* California Land-Use Planning Series: Save San Francisco Bay Association, 1961–1986, Regional Oral History Office, Bancroft Library, University of California, Berkeley, 1987, https://digitalassets.lib.berkeley.edu/roho/ucb/text/save_sfbay.pdf.

83   *he simply replied: "No":* "Nick Petris SF BCDC Part 1," LeroyDong, YouTube, September 10, 2007, https://www.youtube.com/watch?v=qZORuYpt1tQ.

Chapter 10

93   *increase in chronically unhoused:* County of Marin Health and Human Services, "Marin County 2013 Point in Time Count Comprehensive Report Findings," 2013, https:// www.marinhhs.org/sites/default/files/files/servicepages/2013_09/2013_point_in _time_count_full_report.pdf; Applied Survey Research, "Marin County 2017 Homeless Count and Survey Executive Summary," 2017, https://www.marinhhs.org/sites /default/files/files/servicepages/2017_07/marin_pit_executive_summary_2017.pdf.

93   *ran an opinion piece:* Barbara Salzman and Marjorie Macris, "Protect Richardson Bay, Remove the Anchor-Outs," *San Francisco Chronicle,* May 2, 2017, https://www.sf chronicle.com/opinion/openforum/article/Protect-Richardson-Bay-remove-anchor -outs-11115436.php.

94   *more than one thousand:* Applied Survey Research, "Marin County 2017 Homeless Count and Survey Executive Summary."

94   *about 15 percent:* Applied Survey Research, "Marin County 2017 Homeless Census and Survey Comprehensive Report."

94 *salary of about $100,000:* Alan Burr, "A Fact-Based Overview of the State of Housing in Our County," *Imagine* 9 (November 2016), https://www.mcf-imagine.com/article /issue-no-9/affordable-housing-in-marin-an-overview.

94 *the department's new anchor-out plan:* City of Sausalito, Sausalito City Council Regular Meeting, June 21, 2016, https://sausalito.granicus.com/player/clip/298?view_id=6& redirect=true.

Chapter 11

100 *Newspapers in Chicago:* "Anarchy! Anarchism! Anarchist!!!," *Labor Enquirer*, September 11, 1886.

Chapter 12

104 *fastest voyage from San Francisco:* Larry Clinton, "The Last, Sad Days of the Galilee," Sausalito Historical Society, September 1, 2021, https://www.sausalitohistoricalsociety .com/2021-columns/2021/9/1/the-last-sad-days-of-the-galilee.

108 *"I'm one of the greatest painters":* "Van Bo: Renaissance Man of Sausalito," pistolstamen, YouTube, September 23, 2017, https://www.youtube.com/watch?v=GNJowXk3cFE.

108 *calling himself Bocasso:* Paul James, "Van Bo Died," *The Sausalito Waterfront Is Changing*, June 23, 2017, http://sausalitoischanging.blogspot.com/2017/06/van -bo-died.html.

Chapter 13

110 *overall number of unhoused:* "Homelessness in Marin: A Progress Report," 2017–2018, Marin County Civil Grand Jury, May 17, 2018, http://marin.granicus.com/Document Viewer.php?file=marin_a46423d8d9981125cea5c37ff0a4cbfd.pdf.

110 *drafted a response:* City of Sausalito, "Response to Grand Jury Report—'Homelessness in Marin—A Progress Report,'" July 29, 2018, https://www.marincounty.org/-/media /files/departments/gj/reports-responses/2017-18/responses/homelessness-in-marin /city-of-sausalito.pdf?la=en.

111 *City Council placed the adoption:* City of Sausalito, Regular City Council Meeting Agenda, July 17, 2018, https://sausalito.granicus.com/player/clip/724?view_id=6&r edirect=true.

112 *Pine Point waterfront neighborhood:* Advance Design Consultants, Inc., and Urban Planners, "Evaluation of Historic Resources in Compliance with the National Historic Preservation Act of 1966 (as Amended): 36 CFR Part 800—Section 106: To Consider the Potential for Historic Resources to Be Affected by the Development of a US Department of Veterans Affairs Medical Research Facility in Sausalito, California," n.d., https://www.cfm.va.gov/realProperty/HRP/MachineShop/NHPA_Eval_of_Historic _Resrcs.pdf.

112 *On top of that:* VerPlanck Historic Preservation Consulting, "Sausalito Citywide Historic Context Statement," prepared for City of Sausalito and the Office of Historic Preservation, October 2022, http://www.verplanckconsulting.com/Sausalito-City wide-Historic-Context-Statement.pdf.

112 *A shipping channel:* Advance Design Consultants, Inc., and Urban Planners, "Evaluation of Historic Resources in Compliance with the National Historic Preservation Act of 1966."

112   *122,000-square-foot warehouse:* VerPlanck Historic Preservation Consulting, "Historic Context Statement: Marinship," prepared for Community Development Department, Sausalito, California, June 2011, https://www.sausalito.gov/home/showpublisheddoc ument/9344/636326254065130000.

113   *seventy-five thousand workers:* April Harper, "Marinship to Marin City: How a Shipyard Built a City," *Found SF*, 2015, https://www.foundsf.org/index.php?title=Marinship _to_Marin_City:_How_a_Shipyard_Built_a_City.

114   *redlining and exclusionary zoning:* VerPlanck Historic Preservation Consulting, "Sausalito Citywide Historic Context Statement."

Chapter 18

147   *"a seaworthy sailor":* Lorenzo Morotti, "Richardson Bay Mariner Found Dead After Boat Fire," *Marin Independent Journal*, November 16, 2020, https://www.marinij .com/2020/11/16/richardson-bay-mariner-found-dead-after-boat-fire/.

Chapter 19

155   *"edge of the channel":* Nikki Silverstein, "Activist Occupies Sailboat in Latest Chapter of Battle for Richardson Bay," *Pacific Sun*, December 3, 2020, https://pac ificsun.com/activist-occupies-sailboat-in-latest-chapter-of-battle-for-richardson -bay/.

Chapter 21

165   *homelessness in California:* US Department of Housing and Urban Development, "The 2020 Annual Homeless Assessment Report (AHAR) to Congress," January 2021, https://www.huduser.gov/portal/sites/default/files/pdf/2020-AHAR-Part-1.pdf; US Department of Housing and Urban Development, "The 2019 Annual Homeless Assessment Report (AHAR) to Congress," January 2020, https://www.huduser.gov/por tal/sites/default/files/pdf/2019-AHAR-Part-1.pdf.

165   *audited the BCDC:* Auditor of the State of California, "San Francisco Bay Conservation and Development Commission: Its Failure to Perform Key Responsibilities Has Allowed Ongoing Harm to the San Francisco Bay," May 2019, https://information .auditor.ca.gov/reports/2018-120/summary.html.

166   *"as mom-and-pop":* Miranda de Moraes, "Pirates of the Bay," *SF Weekly*, June 10, 2021, https://www.sfweekly.com/archives/pirates-of-the-bay/article_4530cc12-03f3-5e3e -b415-b15c7e93fde2.html.

166   *increased the number of seizures:* Richardson's Bay Regional Agency Board of Directors, "Richardson's Bay Regional Agency Transition Plan," June 11, 2020, https://rbra .ca.gov/files/7adfcda86/Adopted+Transition+Plan+-+Final.pdf.

166   *On any given day:* US Department of Housing and Urban Development, "The 2020 Annual Homelessness Assessment Report (AHAR) to Congress," December 2023, https://www.huduser.gov/portal/sites/default/files/pdf/2020-AHAR-Part-1.pdf.

167   *the state's governor:* Office of Governor Gavin Newsom, "California Clears More Than 1,250 Homeless Encampments in 12 Months," September 2022, https://www.gov .ca.gov/2022/08/26/california-clears-more-than-1250-homeless-encampments-in -12-months/.

Chapter 22

168 *city council meeting:* Sausalito City Council meeting, February 5, 2021, https://sausalito
.granicus.com/player/clip/1098?view_id=6&redirect=true.

169 *possible legal challenges:* Martin v. City of Boise, 920 F.3d 584 (9th Cir. 2019), https://
law.justia.com/cases/federal/appellate-courts/ca9/15-35845/15-35845-2019-04-01
.html.

171 *"very difficult to detect":* Tim Henry, "The End of the Anchor-Out Era, Part 3," *Latitude 38*, February 25, 2022, https://www.latitude38.com/lectronic/the-end-of-the
-anchor-out-era-part-3/.

174 NOTICE TO VACATE: Sausalito/Marin County Chapter of California Homeless Union v.
City of Sausalito, 522 F. Supp. 3d 648 (N.D. Cal. 2021), https://casetext.com/case
/sausalitomarin-cnty-chapter-of-cal-homeless-union-v-city-of-sausalito.

Chapter 23

175 *"Clearing encampments can cause":* Centers for Disease Control and Prevention,
"Interim Guidance on Unsheltered Homelessness and Coronavirus Disease 2019
(COVID-19) for Homeless Service Providers and Local Officials," August 6, 2020,
https://www.cdc.gov/coronavirus/2019-ncov/community/homeless-shelters/unshel
tered-homelessness.html#prevention%5C.

175 *The court agreed:* Sausalito/Marin County Chapter of California Homeless Union v.
City of Sausalito, 522 F. Supp. 3d 648 (N.D. Cal. 2021), https://casetext.com/case
/sausalitomarin-cnty-chapter-of-cal-homeless-union-v-city-of-sausalito.

177 *sewage leaked into the estuary:* Lorenzo Morotti, "Sausalito Sewage Spill Unloads Nearly
100K Gallons," April 13, 2021, https://www.marinij.com/2021/04/12/sausalito
-sewage-spill-unloads-nearly-100k-gallons/.

Chapter 24

178 *chainsaw ripping through the cabin:* "Man Living on Boat on Richardson Bay
Arrested—April 2, 2021," *Pacific Sun*, YouTube, April 13, 2021, https://www.you
tube.com/watch?v=fHEc-XnOPGc&t=5s.

179 *"refused to give up":* Nikki Silverstein, "Tensions Rising on Richardson Bay as Police
Arrest Man Living on Boat," *Pacific Sun*, April 14, 2021, https://pacificsun.com
/tensions-rising-on-richardson-bay-as-police-arrest-man-living-on-boat/.

Chapter 27

195 *met at a city council meeting:* City of Sausalito, Regular City Council Meeting Agenda,
September 28, 2021, https://sausalito.granicus.com/player/clip/1262.

Chapter 28

200 *"babblers and yellers":* Savy Behr, "Tent City," *Tam News*, October 24, 2021, https://
thetamnews.org/22404/features/tent-city/.

Chapter 29

204 *living in cars and RVs:* Applied Survey Research, "2021 Marin County Homeless

Vehicle Count," February 25, 2021, https://www.marinhhs.org/sites/default/files/files/marin_vc_2021_4.14.21.pdf.

204 *an informal survey:* Lauren Hepler, "The $2 Million Encampment: How a California Yacht Town Became a Homeless Battleground," *San Francisco Chronicle*, October 29, 2022, https://www.sfchronicle.com/bayarea/article/sausalito-homeless-encampment-17531723.php.

Chapter 30

206 *clocked at 56 miles per hour:* City of Sausalito, "Recap of the First Storm of the Season," October 29, 2021, https://www.sausalito.gov/Home/Components/News/News/5980/509?backlist=%2Fdepartments%2Fadministration%2Fcity-clerk.

206 *Throughout Sausalito:* Natalie Hanson and Adrian Rodriguez, "Marin Mops Up After Deluge from Storm," *Marin Independent Journal*, October 26, 2021, https://www.marinij.com/2021/10/25/live-updates-flood-watch-continues-as-storm-impacting-marin-persists/.

206 *homes went dark:* City of Sausalito, "Storm Brings Power Outages and Flooding to Sausalito," October 24, 2021, https://www.sausalito.gov/Home/Components/News/News/5968/457?seldept=2&npage=10&arch=1.

207 *details of what occurred:* City of Sausalito, Sausalito Regular City Council Meeting, October 26, 2021, https://sausalito.granicus.com/player/clip/1276?view_id=6&redirect=true.

207 *erect a storage shed:* Giuseppe Ricapito, "Sausalito Lifts Demolition Threat over Homeless Camp Structure," *Marin Independent Journal*, November 5, 2021, https://www.marinij.com/2021/11/05/sausalito-lifts-demolition-threat-over-homeless-camp-structure/.

208 *rancid liquid:* Giuseppe Ricapito, "Sausalito to Move Homeless Campers from Sewage Risk," *Mercury News*, November 20, 2021, https://www.mercurynews.com/2021/11/20/sausalito-to-move-homeless-campers-from-fecal-spillage-risk/.

208 *the city had acknowledged:* Nikki Silverstein, "Sausalito Admits Fecal Contamination at Homeless Encampment," *Pacific Sun*, November 19, 2021, https://pacificsun.com/sausalito-fecal-contamination/.

209 *one was certainly accurate:* Giuseppe Ricapito, "Sausalito Declares Emergency After Homeless Camp Explosion," *Marin Independent Journal*, February 10, 2022, https://www.marinij.com/2022/02/10/sausalito-declares-emergency-after-homeless-camp-explosion/.

209 *emergency order chastised:* City of Sausalito, "State of Emergency Declared After Fire, Explosion at Encampment," February 10, 2022, https://www.sausalito.gov/Home/Components/News/News/6138/457.

209 *"violence and threats of violence":* City of Sausalito, "Proclamation of a Local Emergency by the Director of Emergency Services," February 10, 2022, https://www.sausalito.gov/home/showpublisheddocument/31015.

209 *claimed to a* Pacific Sun *reporter:* Nikki Silverstein, "Sausalito Homeless Residents Make Serious Allegations Against Urban Alchemy," *Pacific Sun*, June 1, 2022, https://pacificsun.com/workplace-violations/.

210 *reached an agreement with the anchor-outs:* City of Sausalito, "Settlement Agreement

and Release," August 26, 2022, https://www.sausalito.gov/home/showpublisheddocu
ment/31825/637970325834770000.

Chapter 32

220 *The neighborhood is situated:* Tenderloin Health Improvement Partnership, "Transforming Health Outcomes in San Francisco's Most Vulnerable Neighborhood,"
American Hospital Association, March 1, 2017, https://www.aha.org/hav/case-study
/tenderloin-health-improvement-partnership.

220 *contains about 3,800:* David Sjostedt, "6 of San Francisco's Most Common Homelessness Questions, Answered: Ask the Standard," *San Francisco Standard*, June 7, 2023,
https://sfstandard.com/2023/06/07/san-francisco-homelessness-questions-answers/.

220 *without housing in San Francisco:* Department of Homelessness and Supportive Housing, "San Francisco Homeless Count and Survey: 2022 Comprehensive Report,"
2022, https://hsh.sfgov.org/wp-content/uploads/2022/08/2022-PIT-Count-Report
-San-Francisco-Updated-8.19.22.pdf.

Chapter 34

229 *"My name is Richard Dream Weaver":* Video interview of Dream Weaver recorded and
provided by Nic Mosher.

Epilogue

237 *Thousands of cities:* Alastair Gee, Julie Carrie Wong, Paul Lewis, Adithya Sambamurthy,
Charlotte Simmonds, Nadieh Bremer, Shirley Wu, Carla Green, Erin McCormick,
Winston Ross, Thacher Schmid, Luis Trelles, Amanda Waldroupe, Joanna Walters,
Daniel Hollis, Sara Lafleur-Vetter, Michael Landsberg, and Logan Newell, "Bussed
Out: How America Moves Its Homeless," *Guardian*, December 20, 2017, https://
www.theguardian.com/us-news/ng-interactive/2017/dec/20/bussed-out-america
-moves-homeless-people-country-study.

237 *"outstretched" in stations:* Giulia Heyward, "NYC Mayor Adams Faces Backlash for
Move to Involuntarily Hospitalize Homeless People," NPR, November 30, 2022,
https://www.npr.org/2022/11/30/1139968573/nyc-mayor-adams-faces-backlash-for
-move-to-involuntarily-hospitalize-homeless-pe.

BIBLIOGRAPHY

Anderson, Nels. *The Hobo: A Sociology of the Homeless Man*. University of Chicago Press, 1923.

Armstrong, Leroy, and J. O. Denny. *Financial California: An Historical Review of the Beginnings and Progress of Banking in the State*. Coast Banker Publishing Co., 1916.

Barker, Malcolm E. *San Francisco Memoirs 1835–1851: Eyewitness Accounts of the Birth of a City*. Londonborn Publications, 1994.

———. *Three Fearful Days: San Francisco Memoirs of the 1906 Earthquake & Fire*. Londonborn Publications, 2005.

Bonsall, Crosby. *What Spot?*, Simon & Schuster, 1963.

Brechin, Gray. *Imperial San Francisco: Urban Power, Earthly Ruin*. University of California Press, 1999.

Cohen, Allen. *The San Francisco Oracle: The Psychedelic Newspaper of the Haight Ashbury*. CreateSpace Independent Publishing Platform, 2011.

Conley, Robert, Jr. *Afrobozodiac*. Self-published, n.d.

Cowan, Robert Ernest, Anne Bancroft, and Addie Ballou. *The Forgotten Characters of Old San Francisco*. Ward Ritchie Press, 1938.

Cresswell, Tim. *The Tramp in America*. Reaktion Books, 2001.

Dickinson, A. Bray. *Narrow Gauge to the Redwoods: The Story of the North Pacific Coast Railroad and San Francisco Paddle-wheel Ferries*. North Pacific Coast Railroad Co., 1970.

Dickson, Samuel. *Tales of San Francisco*. Stanford University Press, 1983.

Dougherty, Conor. *Golden Gates: Fighting for Housing in America*. Penguin Press, 2020.

Edelman, Peter. *Not a Crime to Be Poor: The Criminalization of Poverty in America*. New Press, 2017.

Geary, Ida. *Marin Trails: A Natural History Guide to Marin County*. Tamal Land Press, 1969.

Geary, Marilyn L. *Marin City Memories: From the Deep South to the Shores of San Francisco Bay*. Life Circle Press, 2001.

George, Henry. *Progress and Poverty: An Inquiry in the Cause of Industrial Depressions, and of Increase of Want with Increase of Wealth: The Remedy* [1879]. Modern Library, 1938.

Gibson, Dorothy E. *Sausalito's Parks, Plazas, Playgrounds, and Benches: The Histories and Stories*. Published by the author, 2017.

Gilliam, Harold. *Between the Devil and the Deep Blue Bay: The Struggle to Save San Francisco Bay*. Chronicle Books, 1969.

———. *San Francisco Bay*. Doubleday, 1957.

Harrington, Michael. *The Other America: Poverty in the United States*. Macmillan, 1962.

Hayton-Keeva, Sally. *Juanita!: The Madcap Adventures of a Legendary Restaurateur*. Sagn Books, 1990.

Heig, James, and Shirley Mitchell. *Both Sides of the Track: A Collection of Oral Histories of Belvedere and Tiburon*. Scottwall Associates, 1985.

Hirschhorn. *History of Marin County, California*. CreateSpace Independent Publishing Platform, 2016.

Hoffman, George Cleborn. *Saucelito-aualito: Legends and Tales of a Changing Town*. Woodward Books, 1976.

Johnson, Susan Lee. *Roaring Camp: The Social World of the California Gold Rush*. W. W. Norton, 2000.

Katz, Michael B. *The Undeserving Poor: America's Enduring Confrontation with Poverty*. Oxford University Press, 2013.

Kerr, Helen B. *Sausalito: Since the Days of the Spanish Dons*. Zone West Press, 1967.

Lewis, Oscar. *San Francisco: Mission to Metropolis*. Howell-North Books, 1969.

Lilley, William, III. *The System of the River: Francis Newlands and the Improbable Quest to Irrigate the West*. Stanford University, Bill Lane Center for the American West, 2019.

Lotchin, Roger W., ed. *Narratives of the San Francisco Earthquake and Fire of 1906*. Lakeside Press, 2011.

Love, Edmund G. *Subways Are for Sleeping*. Harcourt, Brace, 1957.

Lyman, George D. *Ralston's Ring*. Charles Scribner's Sons, 1937.

Matters, Simple. *The Gift of the Priceless Pearl: The Beginning of a Legacy*. Self-published, 2013.

Merriam, C. Hart. *The Dawn of the World: Myths and Tales of the Miwok Indians of California* [1910]. University of Nebraska Press, 1993.

Miller, Robert Ryal. *Captain Richardson: Mariner, Ranchero, and Founder of San Francisco*. La Loma Press, 1995.

Nelsen, T. J. *Houseboats, Drugs, Government and the 4th Estate*. Dorrance Publishing, 2015.

Odell, Rice. *The Saving of San Francisco Bay: A Report on Citizen Action and Regional Planning*. Conservation Foundation, 1972.

Pimpare, Stephen. *The New Victorians: Poverty, Politics, and Propaganda in Two Gilded Ages*. New Press, 2004.

———. *A People's History of Poverty in America*. New Press, 2008.

Rothstein, Richard. *The Color of Law: A Forgotten History of How Our Government Segregated America*. Liveright Publishing, 2017.

Scott, Mel. *The Future of San Francisco Bay*. University of California at Berkeley, Institute of Governmental Studies, 1963.

Scott, Stanley. *Governing a Metropolitan Region: The San Francisco Bay Area*. University of California at Berkeley, Institute of Governmental Studies, 1968.

Smith, Dennis. *San Francisco Is Burning: The Untold Story of the 1906 Earthquake and Fires*. Plume, 2006.

Soulé, Frank, John H. Gihon, and James Nisbet. *The Annals of San Francisco*. Appleton, 1855.

Stanford, Sally. *The Lady of the House: The Autobiography of Sally Stanford*. Putnam, 1966.

Starr, Kevin. *California: A History*. Modern Library, 2005.

Thalman, Sylvia Barker. *The Coast Miwok Indians of the Point Reyes Area*. Point Reyes National Seashore Association, 1993.

Tracy, Jack. *Sausalito: Moments in Time: A Pictorial History of Sausalito's First One Hundred Years, 1850–1950*. Windgate, 1983.

Trattner, Walter I. *From Poor Law to Welfare State: A History of Social Welfare in America*. Free Press, 1994.

Vanderstaay, Steven. *Street Lives: An Oral History of Homeless Americans*. New Society Publishers, 1992.

Wollenberg, Charles. *Golden Gate Metropolis: Perspectives on Bay Area History*. University of California at Berkeley, Institute of Governmental Studies, 1985.

———. *Marinship at War: Shipbuilding and Social Change in Wartime Sausalito*. Western Heritage Press, 1990.

ABOUT THE AUTHOR

JOE KLOC IS A REPORTER AND SENIOR EDITOR AT *HARPER'S MAGAZINE*, where he was a finalist for the 2019 National Magazine Award for Feature Writing. His work has also appeared in the *New York Times Magazine*, *The Guardian*, *New York* magazine, and the *New York Review of Books*.